Augusta National Golf Club

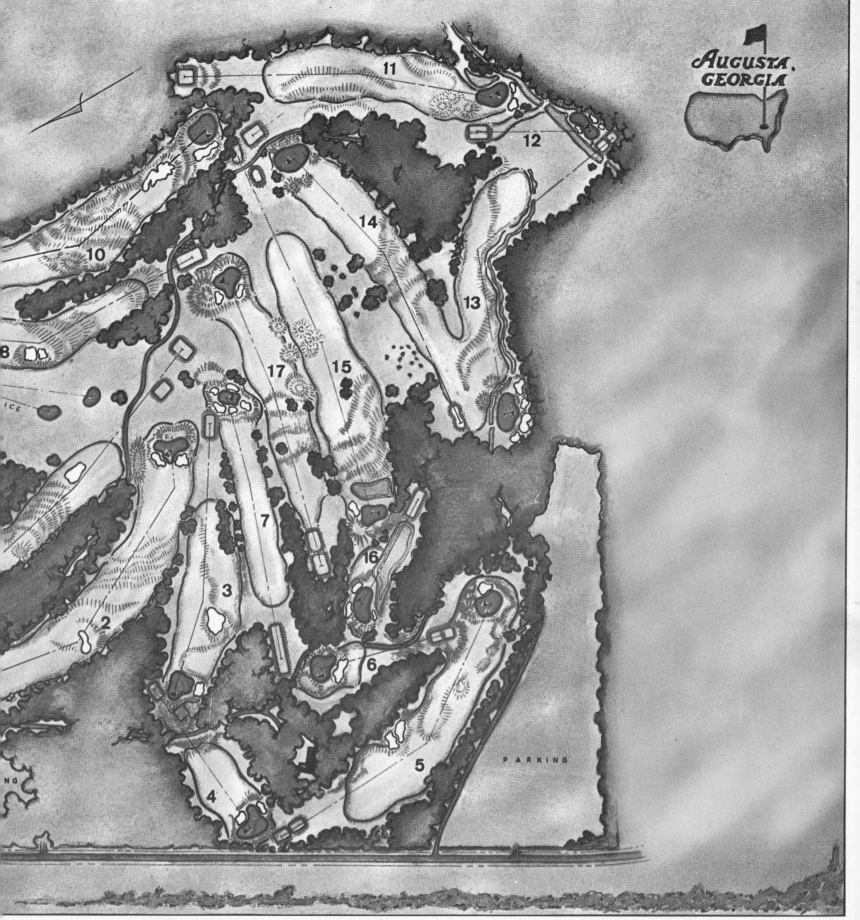

Augusta, Georgia

Augusta National Golf Club

The Masters

The Masters

Augusta Revisited:
An Intimate View
by Furman Bisher

Oxmoor House, Inc.
Birmingham

ISBN: 0-8487-0416-9
Library of Congress Catalog Card Number: 76-14110
Printed in the United States of America
Copyright © 1976 by Oxmoor House, Inc.
P.O. Box 2463, Birmingham, Alabama 35202
All rights reserved
First Edition

Oxmoor House, Inc., is the Book Division of
The Progressive Farmer Company:

Eugene Butler   *Chairman of the Board and Editor-in-Chief*
Emory Cunningham   *President and Publisher*
Vernon Owens, Jr.   *Senior Executive Vice President*
Roger McGuire   *Executive Vice President*
Leslie B. Adams, Jr.   *Vice President and Director of Book Division*

Conceived, edited and published by Oxmoor House, Inc.,
under the direction of:

John Logue   *Editor-in-Chief*
Ann H. Harvey   *Managing Editor*
Robert L. Nance   *Production Manager*
Philip T. Sankey   *Designer*

Grateful acknowledgment is made for permission
to use the photographs on the following pages:

Photographs on pp. ii-iii, v, vi, 2-3, 4, 5, 6, 8, 14,
    15 (lower), 16 (lower), 18, 23, 26, 31, 32 (upper
    left) (lower), 33 (upper left) (upper right), 34-35,
    40, 49 (lower left) (lower right), 50, 56, 57, 58,
    59, 66, 67, 73, 74, 79, 82-83, 84, 90, 91, 92, 93,
    94, 102, 104, 105, 106, 115, 116, 117, 124, 126,
    131, 138, 139 (upper) (lower left), 146-147, 148,
    149, 154, 160, 161, 162, 163 (upper), 164, 172
    — Frank Christian, Photographer

Photographs on pp. 15 (upper), 16 (upper), 32
    (upper right), 36, 43, 47, 48, 60, 99, 118, 128,
    139 (lower right), 140, 163 (lower), 168
    — Fitz-Symms of Augusta

Photographs on pp. 7, 33 (lower)
    — Floyd Jillson

Photographs on pp. i, 17, 49 (upper),
    125, 127, 145, 150
    — Leonard Kamsler

Photograph on p. 157
    — United Press International

Grantland Rice (L), the famed sportswriter, Bobby Jones (R), and friend striding down 10th fairway in 1934.

One True, Authentic American Hero

How do I write a tribute to Bob Jones?

What license have I to write a tribute to Bob Jones? I feel as unqualified as a caddy trying to tell a great player what a beautiful shot he has hit.

I do this because I feel this compulsion. In the months of preparing this book, I have read time and again of the esteem in which Bob Jones was held. It transcended the mere boundaries of Sport.

I think not of him in terms of "athlete." Not as one thinks of Ruth or Dempsey or Londos or Fats Henry of his age, or Butkus or Mikan or Musial of ages later. They sweated. They were involved in physical stress.

Bob Jones was on a plane above this. It seems almost irreverent to think that he sweated and became rumpled as he performed. Always in pictures of him in competition on the course he appeared supremely cool, everything in place and in control. "Sportsman" befits this image. He performed as much with his mind as with his body.

The Masters lives in his image. The atmosphere that Clifford Roberts and the membership of Augusta National have created and maintained is the atmosphere in which Bob Jones moved.

I was privileged to know him, but it was late. His show was over. I could only read of it and hear him talk of it. He was hospitable, considerate, engaging, indulgent, witty, and deft in handling the blade of the critic. To have him call your name as he spoke to you from his cart on the course gave you a very special feeling. I am quite certain, however, that maudlin display offended him.

That the Masters shall be forever played in his spirit is a thought that makes his absence less rending. For he is there.

America gets rather careless in its use of *hero* in its moments of high elation. But if there has been one true, authentic American hero, it was Bob Jones.

He needs no tribute from me. But I wanted to say it, and it is said.

Furman Bisher

The Masters Field of 1935
Back Row: Walter Hagen, Horton Smith, Phil Perkins, George Jacobus, Byron Nelson, Al Espinosa, Errie Ball, Jug McSpaden, Denny Shute, Freddie Haas, Al Watrous, Leo Diegel, Gene Kunes, Dick Metz, Willie Klein, John Dawson, Jack Munger, Wilford Wehrle, Gus Moreland, Ky Laffoon, Ralph Stonehouse.
Center Row: Andy Kay, Tommy Armour, Jules Huot, Bill Schwartz, Bill Mehlhorn, Freddie McLeod, Jock Hutchison, Frank Walsh, Craig Wood, Ray Mangrum, Clarence Clark, Jimmy Hines, Mike Turnesa, Joe Turnesa, Vic Ghezzi, Abe Espinosa, Walter Kozak, Pat Tiso.
Front Row: Jimmy Foulis, Tony Manero, Bobby Cruickshank, Gene Sarazen, Charley Yates, Paul Runyan, Bobby Jones, Olin Dutra, Johnny Farrell, Willie MacFarlane, Jimmy Thomson, Harry Cooper, Johnny Revolta, Henry Picard.

2

Above: Bobby Jones follows through on 1st tee in 1935. Tommy Armour, Walter Hagen, and Gene Sarazen (L to R) form a gallery of the three most notable professionals of the time. Manor Clubhouse is in the background.

Opposite page: Barefoot, trouser legs rolled up to the calves, Claude Harmon wades into the pond fronting the 15th hole and saves par with this recovery shot in the second round in 1948.

Sam Snead putting on 18th green, before adopting the sidesaddle stance of his later years.

Above: Ralph Guldahl putts out, a relatively disinterested gallery of two reflecting his non-challenging position. He later won the Masters in 1939.

Right: Henry Picard, 1938 champion, takes a practice swing, with 1st fairway stretched out behind him.

Ben Hogan watches the flight of a wedge shot in 1953, when he won the Masters, U.S. Open, and British Open. His performance in that Masters has been called "the finest four rounds in the first 100 years of golf."

Augusta National...a Reverie

Augusta National in the spring, azaleas in full glory, the giant live oak standing like a sentry.

"... Hanging above and about you
in all their wax-leafed elegance are
the 64 Southern Magnolias that
form the longest drive in golf ...."

The route is old and familiar and
memorized. The canal by the ancient red
brick textile plant pictured in the
geography books ... the Dixie Vim filling
station ... "Slick Taylor Seat Covers"
(Slick seems to have been there longer
than anybody else for his sign is sadly
faded) ... Free Will Baptist Church ...
Bowman Safe & Lock Co.... and then
Julian Smith Park, just before you reach
the lake, where the true Southern
Bar-B-Q is held each year. Across the lake
you come to the chiropractor with the
office in his home ... the cut-rate gas
place ... then the Burroughs building ...
Sans Souci Apartments ... and Scottish
Rite Temple on the right. The Club
fence, bordered by a tall hedge, springs
up on the left, and there's the sign,
"Service Entrance."

Directly in front of the main gate,
across Washington Road, is The Green
Jacket Restaurant. It's new, and it must
rankle the dignity of the old guard. Then
appearing like some huge tunnel before
you as you guide your car between the
two white brick columns that serve as
gate anchors, hanging above and about
you in all their wax-leafed elegance, are
the 64 Southern Magnolias that form the
longest drive in golf — two-tenths of a
mile from the commonplace of
Washington Road on the outside to the
subdued elegance and the seducing
beauty of America's shrine of golf. You
are standing now at the door of Augusta
National Golf Club, its heart and its focal
point, the old manor house that once
served the plantation that was the South's

9

first nursery. The flagpole stands in the grassy centerpiece like a huge spike rising out of the ground. It is bare. Not a swatch of cloth to flutter from its height.

All about is silence, the stillness that comes with summer disuse. The world seems to have come to a dead stop inside these grounds. It will be so until mid-October when members return; and in the spring, as if by some official act of Golf and by universal acclamation, this land will come awake in its most glorious emergence known as the Masters. Then in mid-May, the quiet comes again. This special world takes its rest in summer. Now, the coolness of a green canopy invites you into the clubhouse.

The first step you take on the forest green carpet brings you face to face with a portrait of Dwight D. Eisenhower, 34th President of the United States. To the left is a matching portrait of Robert Tyre Jones, Jr. A bronze plaque by the reception office memorializes those especially involved in the beginning of Augusta National. "Original Planning 1930," is embossed upon it with admirable reserve. "Organization Committee: Clifford Roberts, chairman; Robert Tyre Jones, Jr., Alfred Severin Bourne, Grantland Rice, William C. Watt."

The first membership, highly restricted — the membership numbers approximately 275 today — could have served as a roll call of classic Americans of arts and letters and those who kept our economy churning: Eugene Grace of steel; Alpheus Beane and E. F. Hutton of stock brokerage; Henry P. Crowell of publishing; Kent Cooper of journalism; Cason Callaway of textiles; Frank Willard of "Gasoline Alley" and Walt and Skeezix; Louis B. Maytag of washing machines; Walton H. Marshall of innkeeping; Melvin Traylor of banking and politics; Devereaux Milburn of polo; G. Herbert Walker of the Walker Cup; Judge John W. Herbert, who played for Rutgers against Princeton in the first college football game, for a cross section. Here they were gathered in America's most exclusive retreat — an affluent but diverse group who had in common their devotion to the game of golf and the cause of privacy.

From the left side of the foyer, all the winners of the Masters gaze out upon you — a gallery of honor banked in a recess newly created in the wall. At the foot of a winding staircase a small metal plate, about the size of a concierge's in a French hotel, discreetly calls attention to "Second Floor Gentlemen Only."

In the spring these steps are busy, but now there are no sounds from above. Closed like an out-of-season shop is the service bar at the head of the stairs around which members, reporters from newspapers and magazines, television's large stable of involvees, and old champions and "Honorary Non-Competing Invitees," as they are designated by the Club — these are former winners of the Masters, U.S. Open and Amateur championships, and the PGA championship annually asked back to supply a touch of flavor and sentiment — gather discussing the rounds of the day. "Arnold Palmer's Scrapbook," bound in dark green leather, an assemblage of pictures and news clippings from the tournaments won by this Pennsylvanian with the magnetic appeal, rests in a wall rack prominently placed. Imprinted on the cover in gold letters is "Presented to Clifford Roberts 1964," significantly the year Palmer became the first to win the Masters four times. He was at his peak as an American folk figure, a strong-striding, steel-wound model of virility, followed at his every step by a thundering, raucous lot of idolaters calling themselves with pride, "Arnie's Army."

To the left, a door opens onto a card room, walls bedecked with pictures of other days when men were younger and pleasure flowed freely. The Club Jamboree of 1946 enjoys a particular indulgence, it having been a year of rejoicing in peace and reunion and a return to the old war-free standards. The Jamboree is an annual in-gathering of members in concentrated congeniality, the rest of the world shut out. Hijinks and whoop-de-do feature the wall art. One picture traps the eye. For one brief flick of a camera's shutter, Beau Jack and Gene Tunney were equals. Both heroes. Jack, the recently unfrocked light-weight champion back on the scene with his popping shoeshine cloth, and Tunney, the gentleman heavyweight champion back from his war. They smile broadly.

A short, steep stairway behind the game room leads to the "crow's nest," a cluster of small bunk rooms just beneath the cupola. Here, a handful of amateur players are quartered during the Masters, for it accommodates just a half dozen. Squint your eyes and peer into the dimness of the past. Some of the forms begin to congeal in the silent eeriness into their images as amateurs in the days when they bunked here as laughing youths. There's Phil Rodgers, portly even as a boy, always the clown, reaching for the fast one-liner, throwing jibes at his pals. Jack Nicklaus, when he bulged at the middle, with his hair cropped almost to the skull like a Luftwaffe pilot in training. Gene Littler — see the freckles come through, glowing with health beneath a greasy-kid look. Ken Venturi, lean and long of neck, dark Italian eyes and the clean Catholic look of an altar boy. Deane Beman, a sprite of a manchild with a laughing face and hair clipped like a brush turned upside down. And Billy Joe Patton, a little more mature than the others when he came here and set the place afire in 1954, losing only to Hogan and Snead, laughing with the eyes behind those spectacles and always chattering. Those were the grand days free of care before these amateurs moved onward, and upward, and outward. Youth seemed

endless. Such young men foresaw no threat in age. They'd kick the traces at night, arise early and unthrobbing in the morning, and one would climb a kind of sailor's ladder, peer out upon the premises through a cupola window, and report upon the weather. It sits well in memory.

From the veranda of the second-floor level, in the museum quietness, there spreads beneath you the earth that is the Masters'. The love, the worship, of golf seems to be everywhere as you stand there absorbed in it yourself. It seems to ooze inside your skin; yet you can't touch it. The veranda gives you a detached view above the lawn upon which, and the spreading water oak trees beneath which, the badged patrons and the honorees of the Masters gather in early April caressed by the richness of a new spring and all its growth. Into this setting your mind is at liberty to place its own cast of personages, those who seem to have become a part of this dramatic lawn: On one of the log benches by the yellow rope that distinguishes between those of the coveted badges and those merely tick-eted, place a pot-bellied eminence, a chain-smoking, elderly Jackie Gleason-sort who clings to his reputation as a putting expert. Nearby station a short, round man, since surrendered to the grave, who fancies himself a gate-crasher of social stature. Make room for the country pro from North Carolina, well schooled in the politics of the Professional Golfers Association. Always include the peddlers, dressed out in their finest for the new season — anything in the golf line. Don't forget the old school hustlers who nursed the golfing tour out of its weanling stage. Scatter odds and ends of the press, a smattering of television persons. And by the tables gaily unbrellaed, seat the ladies, colorful in their spring outpouring and showing more leg and thigh than during the winter just endured. But not as much since the atrocity of pantsuits was brought down upon us.

To the left, further behind the yellow rope, sits the Trophy Room, largely inhabited by members and wives and guests, governors and senators and influential foreign visitors, officials of golf in other parts of the world. Called the Trophy Room because some trophies are kept here, but only a few. Mainly, as you see, shading out the reflection with your hand at the picture window, it is the Trophy Room because Bob Jones' golf clubs are held in covenant here. Flanking a fireplace are two glass-enclosed wall cases of them, those oddly shaped blades and shafts that give more the impression now of ancient garden tools. And, of course, among them the immortal Calamity Jane, his treasured putter.

On the lower side of the Manor Clubhouse, as it is referred to, a second clubhouse was opened in 1962 to accommodate the expanding necessities, and in it a large area simply called the Grill Room where the players are fed and men of affairs at the Masters gather also to eat, to drink, and to lounge. The walls are put to the purpose of honoring the memory of some of the deceased founders and early members of the Club. Their likenesses hang in portrait, but no attention is called to their identities nor their eminence. Their profiles would have been familiar in *Time, Life, Delineator,* and especially *Fortune* and *Forbes* in the age of Coolidge and FDR.

Through the windows of the Grill Room you see the tables unclad. The inside is shadowy on this overcast, summery day, but as your eyes wander about the lifeless room and your imagination runs free, figures indeed do begin to take shape. Suddenly, there appears before you a T-shaped feasting board dressed out for dinner, and in all their green-jacketed glory, the champions of Masters past take their places for their annual exclusive. The dinner was a suggestion out of the

mind of Ben Hogan. "Have all the champions gather each year on Tuesday night before the tournament and drink and eat and talk of old times," he said. "Always, the defending champion shall be the host." And so it came about.

"Just to be invited to the Champions Dinner," as Bob Goalby said, "is worth winning it alone."

Look carefully, and there before you sit Byron Nelson, Ralph Guldahl, and Gene Sarazen, patriarchal champions of the group; and Gary Player, the host as winner in 1974; Jack Nicklaus, who is about to become the first five-time winner; and the only non-champion, Clifford Roberts, composing the head of the T.

Down the right side, all smiling in obvious response to a photographer's coaching, sit Arnold Palmer (now transmitting that mellowing gentleness that comes of graceful aging), Charles Coody, Tommy Aaron, Bob Goalby, Herman Keiser (known as the "Missouri Mortician"), Doug Ford, Billy Casper (now off his diet of buffalo meat and papaya juice), Claude Harmon (who chose wisely the one tournament he should win in all his life), and Jack Burke, Jr. (still too young of face to have won 19 years ago).

And to the left of the head table sit Jimmy Demaret, Sam Snead, Cary Middlecoff, Art Wall (the only champion who never defended, downed by an infected knee), Henry Picard, Gay Brewer, and George Archer. The notable absentee is the man who caused it to be. Ben Hogan is missing, apologetic and on the surface overwhelmed by the urgency of his manufacturing business in Fort Worth but, in reality, belabored by the increasing restrictions brought on by a stiffening knee.

The only non-facial deference to the years is related to the hue of the green in their jackets. Though Casper's victory was not the most recent, the green in his coat is brightest. Nelson's, Sarazen's, and

Guldahl's the darkest. The tablecloths are angel white, each place set with seven pieces of silver, the serving plates bordered, naturally, in green. During the week, the foreign players also will be dined in like splendor, and later the amateurs. The clock above the table shows the time to be four minutes until eight o'clock. It is about the dining hour. The scene fades and the tables sit there again, stark and unclad.

Standing on this vast terrace, the lawn not up to spring standard, bare in some places beneath the huge water oak trees that steal the sunlight, you feel a vast incompetence in your effort to appreciate the history, the grandeur, the greatness of those who have stood on this ground before you, and to absorb what all of this has come to mean in terms of golf. Across the vast expanse, rising still elegantly above the pines, is the upper thrust of the one-time Forest Hills Hotel to remind you of the past. Now it is a Veterans Administration hospital.

The cottage to the left of the 10th tee — a "cottage" in name only — bears a replica of the American eagle above its entrance, for this is "Ike's Cottage." Was when he was General of the Army, President, and former President, and still is. A gaslight burns eternally on the lawn out front. Just below is the cottage that was Bob Jones' to the last of his dwindling days in residence here. There was a custom once in which the leader of each day's round came by to pay his respects, and in turn to be emotionally humbled by this courageous man who refused until no longer mobile to give in to the disease that ravaged his handsome body and features. They shuffled in, those leaders, like schoolboys, hats in hand, to shake the gnarled hand that he offered and to be honored in his bathrobed presence.

He WAS the Masters, and these were his grounds, and this golf course is his outdoor monument. You can stand there until tears well up taking it in with your eyes and cursing the fate that caused such to befall so admirable a sportsman. The disease was called "syringomyelia." You can look it up.

"Is there no cure for it?" I asked him one day many years ago.

"Oh, yes," he said.

"Well, for heaven's sake, what?"

A wry smile crept across his face, then giving ground to sags and wrinkles.

"Death," he said.

Above: Masters Club Dinner, 1972, the year Charles Coody hosted as defending champion.

Left: Ed Dudley, first professional at Augusta National, also once president of the PGA, works on a putter in his shop.

Below: Gene Sarazen, Horton Smith, Byron Nelson, Jimmy Demaret, and Ralph Guldahl (L to R) stroll across the 1st tee trying to look unposed.

Above: The view from the upper deck, reserved for "Gentlemen Only," surveying the terrace lawn from the veranda on the second floor of the Manor Clubhouse on a typical day at the Masters.

Left: Lawson Little, at the height of his career, strolls off 10th tee after a drive.

Above: A panoramic view of the 15th hole, where many a tournament hope has come to its watery grave in the pond in the foreground.

Right: Horton Smith, first two-time champion, putting on 2nd green in one of his winning years.

Opposite page: Johnny Miller playing the 9th hole on Sunday, 1975, his gallery on point in this exciting finishing round; the shoot-out among Miller, Jack Nicklaus, and Tom Weiskopf was won by Nicklaus.

Jones...the Soul of It

Bobby Jones strokes a drive in one of the earlier years, his handiwork studiously followed by one of his professional contemporaries.

"Will Ye No' Come Back Again?"

Robert Tyre Jones, Jr., made his first
association with golf at the age of six. A
man named Fulton Colville, practicing
chip shots in front of the boarding house
where the Joneses had taken summer
quarters at East Lake, noticed him sitting
on the porch steps watching and
addressed him: "Would you like to hit
some, sonny?"

After a few attempts, made shyly and
awkwardly, for he was a scrawny child,
little Bobby was favored with a gift.
Fulton Colville drew an old cleek — that's
something between a putter and a two-
iron — from his bag and handed it to him,
and so the legendary voyage into golf was
launched.

Fulton Colville's role in it was only as
a walk-on, but Bob Jones later said,
"Something inspired him to give me that
club. I didn't have any interest in golf
before then."

It wasn't long before the Jones boy was
out on the golf course at East Lake
Country Club banging his little cleek
around along with his parents. East Lake
is only six miles from the center of
Atlanta, but in those times it was a
summer retreat for the cityites, a colony
surrounded by forest and enveloped by
solitude, perhaps a setting you would
expect in one of Scott Fitzgerald's vintage
stories. Businessmen placed their families
in quarters for the season — the Joneses
chose a Mrs. Meador's — and joined them
by trolley that ran out from downtown. It
was there, under the guidance of an immigrant Scottish golf professional named
Stewart Maiden, that little Bobby Jones
learned the fundamentals of the game
that transformed him from a scrawny kid
into an epic of sport and an international
personality, a blessing for which he paid

his dues to game and society times over.

He became at one and the same time the symbol of the Southern Gentleman and the American Sportsman. Clifford Roberts has said of him, "We never have had an athlete who came close to matching Bob Jones in popularity." It was this popularity that became the cornerstone of Augusta National Golf Club and the Masters golf tournament. It bordered on a kind of sainthood, unofficial but unwavering.

Author Paul Gallico turned his back on sportswriting for fiction with a bittersweet fare-the-well. He wrote a book which bespoke his disillusionment with the games and the people he had covered, but one of these was not Bob Jones, of whom he said, "I have found only one who could stand up in every way as a gentleman and a celebrity, a fine, decent human being, and one who never once since I have known him has let me down in my estimate of him."

Robert Tyre Jones the Golfer was not a "Jr." in the technical sense of familial procedure. His father made him so in defiance of custom because Robert Purmedus Jones regretted not having been named for his father. He passed on to his son the name of his grandfather, staunchly oblivious to the rule that dictates such a christening falls under the heading of "II."

They were the Joneses of Canton, Georgia. They originated in that small town 40 miles north of Atlanta and were in the mercantile business, graduating into textiles before the family became dazzled by the city lights of Atlanta. There, offspring Robert P. became an attorney. For many years he served as general counsel for Atlantic Steel Company. Being an only child, little Robert and his dad became great pals. Mutual admirers. "The Colonel," Bob called him,

as did most of those close to his father. And The Colonel was always there in the gallery when Bob was playing one of his major tournaments. Young Bob dedicated his book, *Golf Is My Game*, to his father and elaborated on their relationship later on. "One of the greatest gifts golf gave me was the enjoyment of many years of playful association with my father," he wrote.

And he DID write it. It was HIS book. Bob Jones would not stand still for a writing "ghost," any third person-first person relationship. When a title once was proposed to him for the old *Saturday Evening Post* with a by-line that would read, "By Bobby Jones as told to . . .," he sniffed. "Makes me sound like a damned illiterate who can't write his own name," he said, and refused.

He was indeed an excellent handler of the language. His literary talent bordered on the Oxonian, finely fundamental and excellently rhetorical. His breadth of interests is brilliantly illustrated in the way he went about his education. He earned a degree in mechanical engineering from Georgia Tech, studied English literature at Harvard, and later whisked through law school at Emory University in a year and a half. He could have been most anything he chose to be, except a sprinter. His feet moved considerably more slowly than his mind, and he often made jokes about his slowness. But then you don't have to run fast to play golf.

As a gentleman sportsman, Bobby Jones was a mountain among hillocks. First, though, he had to learn his lessons himself, and the miracle of it is that he survived to adulthood through a petulant youth of club-throwing, pouting, and childish tantrums that embarrassed partners and rivals. And once, if you can believe it, stalked out of a tournament at the holy of holies, St. Andrews. But once reformed, his reformation was as enduring as it was drastic.

In one of the U.S. Opens he entered a forest to play one of his errant drives. Emerging a few minutes later, he signalled that he was penalizing himself one stroke. The ball had moved as he was addressing it, and the rule clearly calls for a penalty, whether the player is being witnessed or not. It was a matter of honor with Bob Jones, and he was flabbergasted when the act drew such a wave of admiration.

"Well," he said, "you might as well have praised a man for not robbing a bank."

When he beat Watts Gunn for the U.S. Amateur championship in 1925, much was made of the fact that it was the only time two members of the same club had ever advanced to the final round. (And it has never happened again.) The fact is, Watts Gunn was there only because Bob Jones had talked his parents into allowing his younger friend to accompany him and The Colonel to Pittsburgh to play the tournament. Even lesser known was the story of an interception that took place on the back stairs of the clubhouse at Oakmont, where the two friends were staying. Watts had met a young lady in Pittsburgh who had aroused his interest. On the night before the championship match, Bob came upon his friend trying to slip down the back stairway for another date with his new friend. "Oh, no, you don't," Bob said. "You're going to march right back up to that room. You'll need all the sleep you can get for tomorrow." And Watts Gunn's date was suddenly broken.

The competitive part of Jones' life came to an abrupt close in 1948, after which he never was able to play golf again. Struck down by some dastardly fate that was of such a cruel disposition as to reach out and trip a mortal it seemed to have judged to have been given too much. The ailment that invaded his person was a rare one that with a creeping mercilessness took away his ability to manipulate his limbs and eventually shriveled him to a withered ruin of the Adonis that he had once been. "Syringomyelia" was its medical name.

Almost 20 years earlier, however, he had assured himself a place in the roll call of golf's immortals. There is no other achievement in sport comparable to winning the U.S. Open, the British Open, the U.S. Amateur, and the British Amateur championships all in the same year. In fact, this Grand Slam has become, at least by the perceived limits of foreseeable years, the Feat Impossible. The economics of golf have seen to that. Amateur players no longer carry that status any longer than it takes to qualify for the professional tour. There is no longer the lure to remain amateur that existed in Jones' day, when the golf professional was still only a few steps removed from the choreman of the shop. But Jones, fortunate to be backed by a well-to-do father, as an amateur accomplished the Grand Slam. Since his time, not one of the professional players has been able to achieve even the "Pro Grand Slam" by winning the Masters, the U.S. Open, British Open, and PGA championship of the USA in one year.

Shortly after Bob Jones completed the improbable foursome by sinking the putt that defeated Eugene Homans on Marion Cricket Club's 11th green, it being their 29th hole of play in the finals of the U.S. Amateur Championship of 1930, his retirement took effect. Retirement had been lying in the back of his mind since 1926, to be executed only when he could find the proper stopping place. Here he was, barely out of college, retiring from competition in golf at the age of 28, removing from the center ring of the game its stellar attraction. The next four years of American golf were to be low in interest without him. For Jones it was simply the halftime in his life.

Those were times when society rode high and the living was opulent. The estate life and Gatsby's era. Sprawling hotel resorts and the rise of the American Plan. Endurance flying and flagpole sitting. Flappers and Clara Bow. The budding of radio and Atwater Kent. Gloomy Gil Dobie and "Hurry Up" Yost. The Volstead Act and gin made in a bathtub. Sinclair Lewis and the Spirit of St. Louis. Yale-Harvard and Albie Booth against Barry Wood. The Charleston and rooftop ballrooms. Crooning. The Stork Club. Electric fans. And hickory shafts.

Clifford Roberts drove up to Knollwood Country Club one day in the middle of the Roaring '20s, presumably in his Pierce-Arrow or Franklin. Knollwood was located in Westchester County, where New York's wealthy went to the country for the weekend. He was a member. Bobby Jones was playing a friendly match at the club that day, and Roberts was pointedly "dropping in" to take a look at this young man of whom he had heard so much. Other details of the day grow vague, but the two were introduced and discovered they had mutual friends, among them an innkeeper named Walton Marshall, who divided his years between the Hotel Vanderbilt in New York and the Bon Air Vanderbilt in Augusta. Neither had the faintest glimmer of a notion at the time, but with this meeting the first seed of the Augusta National Golf Club was sown.

"Our paths crossed several times after that. I saw Bob play in several tournaments. One I recall distinctly was the National Amateur at Baltusrol when he lost in the final round to George Von Elm," Clifford Roberts said. It happened that Roberts was president that year of the Baltusrol Country Club, near Springfield, New Jersey.

Roberts dealt in investments and securities. Therefore, his life ran to the monied interest, and he turned up at those fashionable addresses frequented by outstanding figures of finance, industry, letters, and politics. One of these was the Bon Air Vanderbilt in Augusta, which in those times registered the finest clientele in America, it is said. As testament, President Taft and J.P. Morgan were frequent guests.

"I had tried Pinehurst two times and had the terrible luck to run into snowstorms both times. Augusta had never heard of snow, and I was encouraged to try this location. It was a choice wisely made, not only for the golf and the climate, but because of the accommodations. Walton Marshall was a notch above your average innkeeper, and the Bon Air was beautifully run. Everyone who came to Augusta stayed at the Bon Air invariably, but, by God, you had to get your reservations in a year in advance. January and February were the height of the season. It was closed in the summer," Roberts said.

"You see, people traveled by train then. Florida was too far, actually wasn't even developed to any great degree. The main purpose of people who came was golf, and Augusta came to fit our needs perfectly. You can step right outside the clubhouse here at Augusta, and you're just 150 feet above sea level. The climate was temperate and the courses were good, and that was the reason Bob spent a good part of his winters over here, playing golf. Conditions were so much better than in Atlanta, which is about one thousand feet higher."

Wherever Bob Jones played, it amounted to an exhibition, as that friendly match at Knollwood had turned out to be. People came out to watch. It was so at Augusta as well. He appeared often at the two courses of prominence then, the Augusta Country Club and Forest Hills, but he simply couldn't play

Bobby Jones shooting out of trouble, the woods skirting the 10th fairway, in what proved to become his last official round in competition in the Masters of 1948.

a round of golf in privacy.

Augusta National, as it turned out, was the product of impulse. Roberts knew that in the back of Jones' mind was the idea of building a golf course to his own specifications and his own taste some time, some place. As they talked of it one day, Roberts blurted out, "Why not here in Augusta?"

A beautiful blend of the minds took place on the spot. It was simply a matter next of finding the proper location, a piece of property that Jones would approve. In the fall of 1930, shortly after Jones had accomplished his Grand Slam, Roberts arrived in Atlanta with a lay of land in mind, requiring only Jones' visual approval and a plan of membership.

There is next this vision of Bob Jones walking from the doorway of the old manor house, which is block-shaped like a fortress, and standing for the first time on the grassy overlook that has since become the terrace lawn of the Augusta National Golf Club.

"The experience was unforgettable," Bob Jones wrote later. "It seemed that this land had been lying here for years just waiting for someone to lay a golf course upon it."

What they had come upon was a gentle, rolling spread of hill and valley with a spring-fed stream that only a near century of preparation could have put in such perfect condition to receive a golf course. The moment of Bob Jones' first view of it came in December, 1930. By the next spring, having heard its ultimate call, the 365 acres of land began to come alive.

While America was still a wilderness, Indians had camped upon this land, attracted by the spring that is the course's source of water, that feeds the lakes and Rae's Creek. De Soto and his marchers are said to have passed through it in their search for the Mississippi River. What the prospective founders of Augusta National Golf Club found there was a former nursery not so tenderly attended for several years. A family of Belgians had settled the property in 1857, and the nursery they created there was the first known in the South. They were of noble heritage. Baron Prosper Jules Alphonse Berckmans, motivating force behind the nursery, was a man of many splendors. Scholar, horticulturalist, landscape architect, botanist, and artist. He had arrived in this country in 1850, having taken his leave of Belgium for political and religious reasons upon which there is no elaboration. He was followed into the nursery business by his two sons, Prosper Jules Alphonse, Jr., and Louis.

The Berckmans' nursery made vast contributions to American horticulture, and the Augusta National Golf Club has gone to great effort to preserve and showcase that bonus that came with its purchase. For instance, all the thousands of miles of privet hedge that grow in the United States can be traced back to the mother hedge that still thrives directly back of the practice tee near where all the monstrous wagons and trailers gather in a television community each week of the Masters. The wisteria vine that seems to writhe out of the ground at the corner of the clubhouse on the terrace lawn is said to be the oldest in the country. The massive oak that stands guard like some arrogant sentry over the entire spread, from clubhouse down the gentle hill to the focal spectating point where the 2nd and 7th greens and the 3rd tee abut, is over 200 years old. Markers are found about the grounds identifying the botanical significance of all the growth of historical note — tree, shrub, and flowering plant.

Old Berckmans had remarried, and at the time of his death in 1910 he willed the property to his young widow instead of the two sons. P.J.A., Jr., and Louis soon left the area and relocated elsewhere. The young widow, having no interest in the nursery, eventually sold the property and its commercial name, "Fruitlands," and for about 15 years prior to its discovery by Clifford Roberts and friends, the acreage had suffered for lack of attention.

One of Augusta's most distinguished industrialists, Fielding Wallace, was appointed to handle the purchase for the Club and eventually became its first secretary. Also, he later became president of the U.S. Golf Association. (Around Augusta, his designation by the man on the street was unique: "The man who runs the Chinese hair factory," for his company imported the hair of Chinese women by the bales and produced mattresses and other products from it.)

As the membership was being formed, one of the first moves made by Clifford Roberts and his group was to search for and locate the two Berckmans sons and induce them to return and spend the rest of their lives on the old family place. P.J.A., Jr., became the Club's first manager. Louis, having fared more prosperously, was able to become a dues-paying member and was appointed the Club's first treasurer. In the process, they made great contributions to the horticultural rejuvenation of the grounds. And so we have a story beginning with a happy ending, and all the peripheral segments of one broad narrative coming together in the fruition of the dream of one man and the vision of another, and for a poignant side effect, the reunion of two brothers with the old soil on which they once bounded about on shoeless feet.

We take our fade-out as Bob Jones makes his solemn pronouncement as to the nature of Augusta National Golf Club and what it was all about at its origin . . . . "Our aim is to develop a golf course and a retreat of such nature, and of such excellence, that men of some means and devoted to the game of golf may find the Club worthwhile as an extra luxury where they may visit and play with kindred spirits from other parts of the nation."

It has been achieved, never veering from course.

"Unless I break down, I hope to participate every year, regardless of how I am putting or where I finish"— Bobby Jones at the first Augusta National Invitation Tournament (which would not become "Masters" officially for four more years), March, 1934.

He WAS the tournament, especially that first year. He made out the first invitation list himself. His name brought the highest price in the Calcutta pool. He made no move but what journalism reported on it. Wherever he went on the course, those men covering the tournament were always close at hand; but it was a different kind of star-media relationship than has developed in the age of television. First, the press entourage was significantly smaller, and Jones knew nearly all of them personally. Also, those writers were privileged to follow close at hand down the fairway and chat with him between shots. When Grantland Rice arrived, their official dean was at hand, and as O.B. Keeler reported in the *Atlanta Journal,* "He [Rice] ruled the tournament as of even greater importance than the National Open." After all, it was the only place in the world where the public could see Bobby Jones play golf anymore. That, as it developed, had not been achieved with ease.

"I had an awful time convincing Bob he should play at all," Clifford Roberts said. "He wanted to be the host and an official. I told him he couldn't invite his friends to a game of golf and not play with them."

People responded. The opportunity to see Bobby Jones play again at $2 a head drew them out in numbers estimated at

With wry expression, Bobby Jones sits (L) on a bench in front of the Manor Clubhouse with Ben Hogan while Jimmy Demaret (L) and Byron Nelson stand by.

3,500, even exceeding expectations. Most of them were gathered around the 1st tee as Jones made his first drive, and they cheered loudly. He wore a checked blue sweater above knickers, with socks to match. Paul Runyan, with whom he was paired, was dressed in a tomato red sweater and matching socks. Jones out-drove the little professional by 40 yards.

"Jones Off in His Putting as Masters Starts." The headline in the *Atlanta Journal* drove directly to the point. Just as Jones had feared, his conduct on the green was erratic. He was playing with an unusual handicap. His treasured companion of all those great years was missing. "Calamity Jane," his putter, had been misplaced, and he'd had to send to Atlanta for a substitute. He three-putted each of the last three greens. His score was 76 on the first round.

Jones finished that first tournament in thirteenth place, tied with Denny Shute, a PGA champion, and Walter Hagen, U.S. Open, British Open, and PGA champion, and the most flamboyant professional of his time, with a score of 294 for the 72 holes. It was to be, as history turned out, Jones' best finish in the tournament created about and for him. Of all the rounds he played in 12 Masters never once did he break par. The scores of his final year, 1948, indicated a deterioration of the game that a man who demanded so much of himself could not long bring himself to tolerate. He shot 75-81-79-79 and finished out of sight at 314. By this time the press had mercifully turned its head and left him to his peace, such as he could find.

During the four years between his retirement from competition and his return in the Masters, Bobby Jones had managed to fill his hours with gainful ventures. Warner Brothers, the film producers, contracted him for a series of instructional shorts with a story, or gag line, including some of the movie idols of the time such as Richard Arlen, W. C. Fields, and Guy Kibbee. The Listerine Company sponsored him in a radio series of golf and how it should be played, teamed with his Boswellian companion, O.B. Keeler. He was syndicated in another instructional form through a regular newspaper column. And the A. G. Spalding Company made his involvement complete when he was contracted to serve the manufacturer of sporting goods for many a lucrative year as a designer and consultant on a line of golf clubs that bore his name. When his career on the course came to an end, he was not, then, left bereft of activity. He also had contacts in the legal profession to develop, and later he bought two Coca-Cola Bottling outlets. And always, always, there was the Masters.

"One of the miracles of it is that a town of some 65,000 can absorb all these people with so little ripple"– Clifford Roberts, 1975.

For several of the earlier years of the Masters, the Bon Air Vanderbilt served the tournament, served Augusta National, and continued to serve a continuing clientele of America's social elite. It was the center of tournament living. Fare was $5 per day, American Plan. Formal dress for dinner was required. Walton Marshall managed on. He was not one to break with, or even allow warpage of, tradition.

Curiously, though, as the golf tournament made gains in popularity, the hotel's prestige lost ground. In no way were these changes of stature related, except for the inescapable fact that expansion of facilities at Augusta National surely siphoned off some of the Bon Air's regular patronage. When World War II broke loose upon the nation, Augusta's face began to change, and many of the old standards and traditions changed with it.

Resort hotels began losing guests to the burgeoning "second-home" movement. Americans began moving about by air. That brought Florida nearer in time, and as the palms, the beaches, and the balmy air became more accessible, so did it become more attractive. The tourist boom broke out, driving the alligators and the Seminoles deeper into the marshes and mosquito country. The piney woods atmosphere of the mid-Southern resorts lost some of its appeal.

The military had taken over the Forest Hills Hotel in Augusta and its golf course during World War II, and civilians never got them back. The Bon Air's demise was less abrupt and dreadfully more painful. It was an awful thing to watch, year to year, its death by deterioration, neglect, and flighty management. It sat there on its hill, a huge white ghost, seeming to cry out for someone to save it. In its halcyon years, natives "down the hill" had gazed upon the Bon Air with awe, watching the great people of America, tycoons, presidents, men of letters and nobility, come and go in their chauffeured livery. Now all barriers were down. The gasping old hotel begged attention. The towns-people moved about its premises with freedom, but found themselves disillusioned, for all the attractiveness and the lure of the glittering personalities were no longer there.

Forest Hills Hotel has now become Oliver General Hospital, a branch of the Veterans Administration. The Bon Air still sits in its crook of Walton Way at the top of the hill, but the world races by it unnoticing. It has become a residential home for senior citizens.

The Hotel Richmond sprang to the fore as the Bon Air began to fade. It was located downtown on Broad Street at the war memorial monument, a place where drummers stayed when the Masters wasn't on. Making no pretense of trying to take the place of the Bon Air in the social life of Augusta, it provided only four walls, a bed, a place to eat, and the necessities of life found in the typical commercial hotel. The Barringers owned it at the time it was cutting its widest swath as a host, but death and estate problems brought it down eventually, too. Now it is closed and has been succeeded by a stunning new modern hostelry called the Executive House. Otherwise, Augusta has become a motel town. The visiting patrons are now decentralized, strung out from Interstate Highway 20, which crosses Washington Road two miles west of Augusta National, to North Augusta, across the Savannah River, and all the way to Aiken, South Carolina.

Then we have the latest form of itinerant resident. He rents. Not a room, but a whole house. He blows in for the week of the tournament. The landlord and family leave town for the week and take a vacation, generously bankrolled by the rental fee. The one-week resident brings in his family, friends, business accounts, or shares with another family. Or as in the case of a tournament player, another golfer and family. Sometimes the house is a classic, one of the columned residences out Walton Way. Sometimes it's a subdivision house without pretension. Sometimes it goes for $1,500 for the week. Nearly every afternoon smoke from charcoal cookery casts a blue pall over the backyard. A few drinks, a steak, to bed, and out to the course early in the morning for the player. For the watcher, a long night, a midmorning brunch, an afternoon of gallerying, and a party in the evening, maybe the annual church Southern Bar-B-Q at the old lodge on the lake Saturday, or the loftier and more formal atmosphere of dinner and dancing at Augusta Country Club.

House rental became popular when the Augusta Chamber of Commerce took this course to satisfy the rooming demands in the years when Augusta was being transformed from a hotel to a motel town, and quarters were short. It has stuck. Some of the tournament players have been renting the same house or in the same residential section for years. Look out the window and Gary Player may be jogging by. Arnold Palmer may be backing out of the driveway. Jack Nicklaus may be standing at the mailbox talking to a one-week neighbor. Just typical American family living with stars in the roles.

... Whitehall Remembered

People drive by that place every day never knowing of its share in the history of golf. It is a silent landmark, saying nothing, revealing nothing of its secret that Bobby Jones once lived there. The address is 3425 Tuxedo Road, dead center in the section of Atlanta where the heart of old Northwest Side society beats. On a turn behind a white spiked fence, the columned mansion sits back from the street, almost out of sight of eyes that would be curious. Where Mr. Jones lived, a Mr. Brown lives now, an implied pseudonymic procession of occupancy as if the address itself seeks its own anonymity. When the Joneses lived there, the mailbox bore a simple black-on-white plate that said "Whitehall." It is not there anymore.

There were three children: Robert III; Clara, named for Bob's mother; and Mary Ellen, named for her own mother. To them "Whitehall" was home, though the name itself had no meaning whatsoever in their lives.

"Dad bought the house from a Dr. Childs, and the name was on the mailbox when we moved there. Dad just never did bother to take it down." Mary Ellen Jones, now Mrs. Carl Hood, wife of a banker, mother of one daughter, car-pooler, member of Lovett School PTA, speaks from a wing chair in the parlor of her home in that part of Atlanta known as Buckhead. "After his operation, we made it a habit to visit him every Saturday afternoon at five o'clock. Have a drink and talk to him about friends and things outside that he had an interest in. We'd go by every afternoon after a Georgia Tech football game and tell him how the team looked and how the new players were working out. He never lost his interest in Georgia Tech, but going to games was out of the question. On the other hand, he kept going to his office nearly every day until about a year before he died."

Mary Malone Jones was in charge of the religious affairs of the family, and being of Irish descent, the children were reared in the Catholic faith. Little Mary Ellen attended parochial school at Christ the King, and one day in her first grade class all the children were asked by their teacher, a nun, to stand and tell of their fathers and what they did. When it came Mary Ellen's turn, she stood and said, "I don't know, but he has an awful lot of blue ribbons, so he must have won something; but my brother and sister have a lot of blue ribbons, too, and they rode horses."

Bobby III and Clara rode in horse shows at summer camp. Kid stuff. Mary Ellen never had such an inclination, nor toward any kind of athletic games, for that matter.

"I never was a golfer, but when Dad was involved in building the Peachtree course, he hired Stewart Maiden, his old teacher, as the professional," Mary Ellen says. "Then he decided Stewart Maiden needed some customers and that I should start taking lessons. So once a week for about a year, I took a lesson from Stewart Maiden, who was not inclined to be very gentle with his instructions. To his outspoken disgust, I was a very poor student.

To paraphrase the title of Dad's book, 'Golf Was NOT My Game.'

"I played golf with him one time in my life, Dad and I against Mother and my brother. A two-ball foursome at Peachtree. The course was still rather new and in an unrefined condition. It was a dreadful experience for him. I put him in poison ivy, honeysuckle, thickets, and brooks, places where he had never been on a golf course. Finally, I was so tired of it all I hauled off without caring and hit a drive on the 4th hole, a par three, and the ball stopped about two feet from the pin. He sank the putt. I said, 'I retire, I quit. I'm finished,' and walked back to the clubhouse."

Of course, most of Bobby Jones' golfing battles had been fought by the time Mary Ellen was born. The Grand Slam had been won. He still played the Masters, but that was not one of the wars, more a walk through the park with old friends and old foes. None of the great conflicts is any part of Mary Ellen's memories. The public's steadfast reverence for her father was there, but even this made no deep impression because she grew up with it.

"They took me to California when I was three months old, when Dad went out there to make those movies. My nurse used to tell me of all the famous movie stars I had met, but I remember none of that." Being the daughter of a celebrated father has made few waves in her life, in other words. "With a name like Mary Jones," she says, wryly, "you can get by without stirring up much attention.

"It was not that way with my brother. Bobby had something to live up to, being the son of Bobby Jones, the great golfer. He always had that shadow hanging over him. It was like being the son of Red Grange and playing halfback. Bobby played well, but never good enough.

"Dad always had this desire for him to qualify for the U.S. Amateur, then finish in one of the positions that would earn him an invitation to the Masters. So one year he qualified for the U.S. Amateur. He flew out to Colorado for the tournament, full of fire and enthusiasm, ready to take that old tiger by the tail. Who does he draw in the first round? A kid named Jack Nicklaus. Bobby never made it to the Masters."

If nothing had yet certified for her the international esteem of her father, his notability, the near sainthood bestowed upon him, the confirmation came in October, 1958, when Mary Ellen was invited along to St. Andrews to witness his acceptance of the Freedom of the City. Just right off, no one was quite certain of the caliber of the honor until it came to light that only one other American had ever received it — Benjamin Franklin. The Joneses flew to London on a flight that almost became a disaster. The plane lost an engine and had to turn back to Gander, Newfoundland, as it approached the point of crisis over the Atlantic. They reached St. Andrews a day behind schedule.

"It was one of the great experiences of my life. The ceremony was a moving thing. I was stunned. Younger Hall was just jammed. We were taken in through the back entrance and seated on a stage. I'll never forget Dad, how he got on that stage and up to the lectern with his two walking sticks. He was determined to do it without any help. It was painful to watch him. I thought he'd never make it, but he did.

"He had worked hard on that speech of acceptance, and it was beautiful. It became quite emotional at the end, and then he and the Provost were seated in a golf cart and they drove down the aisle through the hall. People were crying and reaching out to touch him, and to touch even us, my mother, my brother, and me. I felt like the Queen of England. Then

30

His competitive wars over, Bobby Jones is caught
sitting cross-legged, smoking a cigar
on this casual day at the Masters.

almost in unison, purely spur of the
moment, I think, they began singing 'Will
Ye No' Come Back Again?' well knowing
that he never would. We walked down
the aisle behind him, and I can still feel
the tingles in my spine. It was moving."

As for the Masters tournament, it was
only a glimmer out there on some distant
horizon to Mary Ellen. She heard of it,
read of it, knew of it as some peripheral
event concerning her family, but her
attendance was rare. "A good deal of the
time, especially when Dad was still
playing, I was away at college. Then I was
married and had other interests and
responsibilities. I do remember one year a
bunch of us in our 20s rented a railroad
car and went to the Masters, but that was
more a big party than it was a junket of
golf. I can't even tell you who won it that
year."

Four years before he died in December,
1971, so crippled he could no longer
endure a journey of even 165 miles to the
Masters, Bob Jones and his Mary gave up
the responsibilities of householding for an
apartment on Peachtree Street. Most of
the last 20 years of his life he required
fulltime attendants who served as valet,
hand servant, nurse, and chauffeur. His
man's man at the end was one of distinguished bearing and manner named Hoyt.
Being virtually immobile at this point,
Jones required constant attention. Hoyt
moved along with him to the apartment,
there to watch over him as he awaited his
appointment with death. Three days
before he passed on, Bob Jones told a
close friend, "If I had known it would be
this easy, I wouldn't have been so
worried about it."

On a cold Saturday morning in
December, Robert Tyre Jones, Jr., died.
Two years later, almost to the day,
Robert Tyre Jones III, only 47 years old,
lurched forward and died of a heart
attack in Nashville, Tennessee. In May,
1975, Mary Malone Jones passed away.
Now only the two daughters are left, and
some destiny has drawn them close. Clara
and Mary Ellen live not more than two
blocks apart, and "Whitehall" is not more
than a mile away.

Above: Bert Yancey agonizes over a putt that failed to drop.

Right: In 1974, Tom Weiskopf plays a recovery shot out of the woods.

Below: Umbrellas provide some color around the 1st tee on a rainy, overcast day at the Masters.

Above left: Hubert Green, a son of Alabama, at the end of a drive in 1974.

Above right: Some of the Old Guard, headlined here by the two Honorary Starters of many Masters, Fred McLeod (in yellow) and Jock Hutchison. That's Clifford Roberts, pioneer of Augusta National, at McLeod's right.

Right: Flashy, many-splendored Doug Sanders comes out of the foliage in 1965.

The 16th green provides a stage for the histrionics of Juan (Chi Chi) Rodriguez, Puerto Rico's premier player.

The Tournament...a Surviving Autocracy

Gary Player climbs the 18th fairway incline backed up by the scoreboard story of his final victorious round of 1974.

"If you don't get an invitation to the Masters, it's like being out of the world for a week."
— Doug Sanders

It was morning yet, but already the day was on the hot side, with a fever of humidity rising from days of persistent thunderstorms. Bob Addie, the columnist of the *Washington Post*, and Toney Penna, the former golf professional who now manufactures clubs, sat in a rental car in a long line waiting to get through the gate at Medinah Country Club near Chicago. The U.S. Open of 1975 was being played.

The cars edged along a few feet at a time. The heat bore down. The mood was right for complaint.

"The USGA could take a lesson from the Masters," Penna said to Addie. "That's the best run golf tournament in the world."

"No," said Addie to Penna, "that's the best run sports event in the world."

Clifford Roberts sits behind his desk appearing owlishly wise and stern. Prepared to render instant changes in strategy and tactics. Just as in a well-ordered regiment on the battlefield, there is no doubt about who is in command. Even the initials on the nameplate of the desk speak out of historical authority: "D.D.E." They stand for Dwight David Eisenhower, a general of the U.S. Army when he enlisted as a member of Augusta National Golf Club, and who later, as President of the United States, brought great prestige to the Club.

When he was on the grounds as President Eisenhower, this office was provided for him in a secluded section of Tournament Headquarters Building. (You'll note a certain unvarnished directness in the naming of objects and buildings about the grounds of Augusta National.)

Roberts now occupies Ike's old office and desk. This is where the Masters inhales and exhales. The buck starts and stops here. However, after 40 tournaments, command was transferred to the hands of member William H. Lane, an affable Texas food executive, during the Masters of 1976.

This is one of the last of the successful autocracies and the main reason the Masters has succeeded, achieved, survived is its autocratic nature. Its despotism is a benevolent one. Everyone who passes through the gates is a guest here, player and spectator, but guests must understand that there are rules. They are subtly presented in the form of suggestions; and if one is not aware of them, it's the only golf tournament in the world that supplies them in published form, entitled "Spectator Suggestions for the Masters Tournament." It's a neat little booklet available all around the course at no charge to the guest.

Some examples of the content read: "No matter how well you may know a player, do not accost him on the golf course. Give him a chance to concentrate on his game.

"Walk — never run. Be silent and motionless when a contestant prepares to execute a stroke. Be considerate of other spectators. Golf is a gentleman's game."

There is a tournament committee called the Improvements Committee, composed of 20 members who are all over the course before, during, and after the tournament, each with an assigned operational category, from litter to scoring. Before the last car has passed out the gate after the Sunday round, they are at work on next year. Within a week after the Masters has ended, they have met as a group and made their recommendations. Course changes take priority. Nature has only the summer to do its work, and it becomes a race with time. The Club closes in mid-May after three days of invitational play for volunteer workers of the tournament, part of their reward for loyal service, whereupon maintenance crews spring onto the points of course revision even as the sounds of the last player's footsteps fade through the pines.

In 1975, for example, hole No. 13 was the object of change. The greens on No. 10 and No. 13 have to be replaced periodically because they receive little sunlight, but this time the change on No. 13 was major. A little hump was being installed on the left side; a drainage problem was solved by creating a swale around the upper rim of the green that would carry water to the sides of rather than across the green — which Roberts said should have been done a long time before — and back on the tee another change was taking place. Drives in 1976 would be struck from a new location tucked away about five feet to the left of the old tee location, and the distance would be stretched from 475 to 485 yards, all of this requiring a little more hook and a little more power as the players attempted to turn the corner. By the time Club members returned in mid-October, it would look as though it had been that way forever.

Little or nothing that may be anticipated, excluding acts of God and nature, is left to chance. And a meticulous record of all changes has been kept since the first entry was made in the Club log in 1934, reading, "CBS Radio provides first radio coverage." A sampling of both the monumental and the minutiae hereby follows:

"1938—Tournament officially called
The Masters."
"1946—Trophy Room and kitchen
built." [For years food had
been sent in by caterers.]
"1947—Magnolia Lane paved."

"1948—First modern restroom built.
. . . Robert Tyre Jones, Jr.,
donates golf clubs."
"1949—Roping of holes for gallery
control begun."
"1950—Bunker built at left/front of
No. 1 green."
"1953—Gate guards first assigned at
Magnolia gate entrance."
"1954—Barber shop opened."
"1956—First telecast (CBS). Television rights $5,000."
"1957—Field cut begun (to 40
players plus ties)."
"1958—Woodshed built. . . . Nelson
and Hogan bridges built and
dedicated."
"1959—Pond filled in front of No. 6
green."
"1960—Blazer buttons first introduced by Freeman Gosden."
[A member who was Amos
of Amos N' Andy.]
"1961—Fourth rain-out."
"1962—Litter control personnel
provided uniforms for
recognition. . . . Lower
locker room facility built."
"1963—Attendance limitations for
number of patrons to
Masters instituted."
"1964—Ponds dyed with calcozine
blue for first time."
"1965—Television studio in Butler
cabin first used."
"1966—Resolution passed making
Robert T. Jones, Jr.,
'President in Perpetuity'. . . .
First time credentials sold
out for Masters."
"1967—Pink dogwood trees planted
on course (500)."
"1968—Built linen room. . . .Televi-
sion blackout lifted in
entirety."
"1971—Sneakers provided scoreboard and standard
operators to reduce noise

factors in operating boards."
"1972—Players' names first carried
on uniforms. . . . Shifted No.
10 tee to left."
"1973—Fifth rain-out."

Security personnel, the Pinkerton men,
are given such specific instructions that
there are no grounds for mistakes, to wit:
"Every Pinkerton man should, whenever
he can, set the pace for others by picking
up trash and placing it in the nearest trash
can"; and "One Pinkerton guard is to be
assigned to the No. 16 tee. His job is to
keep spectators off the tee and off the
small bridge to the left of the front of the
tee." Any questions?

One of the rare treats of journalism is
the annual opening of the Masters press
release season, which occurs in January
with an announcement that season tickets
are now being offered, priced at $35.
Each news release originates at the desk
of Clifford Roberts and bears his precisely conservative, properly phrased,
drawing room American English without
variation. Factual, direct, sometimes
stilted — nevertheless, a collection of
them forms an interesting running diary
of the life and times, ups and bumps, and
joys and bereavements of the Masters.

For instance, this entry the year after
Jack Nicklaus won his first tournament:
"This year's list includes one new Lifetime Invitee, Jack Nicklaus, 1963 Masters
champion."

Running to age, as the membership of
the Club does, the passing of old champions and past performers is duly noted
with eulogy and sadness. From the bulletins of 1963 comes this bereaved entry:
"This year the Masters is to be played for
the first time without Horton Smith. Also,
for the first time the Masters Club will
hold its annual dinner without Horton
present. His death, which occurred October 14, 1963, eliminated our first Masters
champion and two-time champion."

Arnold and Ike, champion and President — Arnold Palmer in the early hours of his first reign as winner of the Masters prepares to tee off in the company of President Dwight Eisenhower and Clifford Roberts on a Monday pleasure round.

None of its vintage qualifiers, no matter how long ago was his triumph, is allowed to pass unnoticed. Drawn from the midst of the bulletins of 1954, this somber entry: "H. J. Whigham, the United States Amateur Champion in 1897, died during the past year," though Mr. Whigham never lifted a club in the Masters.

The pleasures of a tournament produced and completed under ideal conditions are not accepted as a right and privilege, but rather all contributing forces, whether for the good or the detriment of the Masters, are duly credited in retrospect, even down to the lowliest plant root on the course. "I do not believe we have ever experienced more exciting competition," the post-tournament summation began one year. "The course never looked better. While there was not as much dogwood and azalea bloom in evidence due to a late spring, this was offset by the presence of flowering peach,

wisteria, and redbud which normally end their blooming period before the start of the Masters."

"Hail Mary, full of grace, the Lord is with thee." Where else but Augusta National? To the general knowledge of all Americans, the PGA and the USGA to this date have never officially recognized the presence or the necessity of nature's wondrous hand, at least in such genuinely admirable, horticultural terms.

When it began, the Masters was nothing masterful at all, but a social affair that politely called itself Augusta National Invitation Tournament. The facilities of the Club were rather restricted, for it had not been constructed with the idea of entertaining the whole membership at one swoop; and so the field of players was kept small, 61 to be exact. Bobby Jones himself made up the first guest list, comprised of golfers he considered "likely to grace the tournament because of their past accomplishments in the game, their present stature, their promise, or even upon my own feeling of friendship for them."

Once was enough of this. Jones realized there was no way he could invite all the friends he chose to favor, God and everybody being aware of the origin of the guest list. This was part of the appeal, being a guest of Bobby Jones. To avoid future embarrassments and to avoid ruffling feelings, a system of qualifications was set up by 1935, to Jones' great relief, and has prevailed, with variations, ever since. Winning itself was not the lone requirement. Certain sporting qualities were also insisted upon.

Since these original requirements, qualification standards for American golfers have undergone a variety of changes, but nearly 30 years passed before the Tournament Committee felt compelled to put the red pencil to the invitation list. When the field bulged to 110 in 1962, some judicious restraints were applied. Invitations to U.S. Open, British Open, PGA championship, U.S. and British Amateur winners subsequently were limited to the winners of the past 10 years, with regret. The accumulation of past champions was assailing the fluidity of operations, cluttering up the course with creaking ancients who had no competitive chance and who had shouldered the tournament field uncomfortably close to that undesirable adjective "sprawling."

A few years later, another cutback went into effect. U.S. and British Open champions and the PGA champion were restricted to five-year invitations, U.S. and British Amateur champions to two, and thus it stands today. The only remaining lifetime invitations go to those who win the Masters. The remainder of the field is made up of the current Ryder Cup team; the Walker Cup and the World Amateur teams in alternating

years; the first 24 finishers in the previous Masters; the first 16 finishers in the previous U.S. Open; the first 8 finishers in the previous PGA championship; semi-finalists in the previous U.S. Amateur; and the winners of PGA tour tournaments classified as "major" for the previous 51 weeks; plus foreign players invited by rule of thumb, but always measured by their performances of the past year or the general excellence of their careers.

As stated by the Tournament Committee, "The foreign section of the field is selected by us on our judgment of ability to provide competition for the U.S.A. players." Usually, the number falls between 15 and 20 each tournament.

It behooves us to pause here and closely inspect this foreign category, for which the Tournament Committee has felt the hot breath of censure periodically. A great deal of it has spewed forth from American players who have fallen short of qualification, but yet feel, on the grounds that they are American, some prior right to an invitation as against some Thai or Korean player. However, Augusta National has painstakingly sought to spread the gospel of American sportsmanship and the Masters and its own club by maintaining international scope. It gives the Masters a special flavor found in no other golf tournament played in America and in few played in any other part of the world. It flashes new personalities upon the American scene with Augusta National's southern magnificence for a background.

The Masters introduced Gary Player to America. It introduced Tony Jacklin to America. It introduced the Englishman with the Dutch name, Peter Oosterhuis, to America. Its earliest invitations were directed mainly to players of the British Empire, but in 1936 two invitations went out to guests of Oriental background, Chick Chin, who was born a Formosan but golfed mainly in Japan, and Torchy Toda, a native Japanese. Chin became the first foreign player to finish in the leading 24. He played the 72 holes in 300 strokes and tied for twentieth place.

Foreign players haven't been making the trip for fun and scenery only. Jim Ferrier of Australia was on his way to a green jacket in 1950 when he stubbed his toe on the last six holes and lost to Jimmy Demaret. Stanley Leonard of Canada went out for the final round of 1959 tied for the lead with Arnold Palmer, shot a 75, and finished in fourth place.

Player became the first foreign winner in 1961, tied after 72 holes in the next year, won again in 1974, and remains the only non-American winner of a Masters; but, Roberto de Vicenzo, the Latin gaucho, came close to winning in 1968. However, he knocked himself out of a play-off with Bob Goalby, the winner, when he, de Vicenzo, signed an incorrect scorecard.

To round out the heroics of the foreign field, a British player, Maurice Bembridge, tied for the course record when he shot a 64 in 1974.

It is seen through these instances that the foreign field has justified its presence in the Masters. But the critics of this policy found fuel for their arguments in the complaint that no American black had ever received an invitation. Patiently, Clifford Roberts explained a number of times that once any black player qualified under one of the variety of standards, he would be invited. Invitations to Americans are earned, not awarded, to reaffirm a point. When four electoral categories were wiped out and replaced by one which included every winner of a regular PGA tour tournament in the field, it seemed the route was widened even more invitingly to any American of any variety who could play golf. The situation reached such a clamorous state in 1973 that 18 members of Congress telegraphed

Augusta National urging that Lee Elder, a black professional whose residence was in Washington, arbitrarily be included in the '73 field.

"We are a little surprised as well as flattered that 18 Congressmen should be able to take time out to help us operate a golf tournament," Clifford Roberts began his one-page reply and reached the crux of it with this sentence: "Before his death, Robert Tyre Jones, Jr., President of the Augusta National, made it clear, in writing, that any black golfer who qualified to play in the Masters would automatically receive the invitation which had been earned."

A little over a year later — 53 weeks, to be exact — Lee Elder won the PGA tournament at Pensacola, Florida. The following April on an overcast Thursday morning, dampened by occasional drizzle, he stepped to the 1st tee at Augusta, struck the most historic drive since Ralph Stonehouse's in 1934, parred the 1st hole, birdied the 2nd, played to a 74 in the company of Gene Littler, and became the first black contestant in the Masters. Unfortunately, he lasted only two days. A 78 on Friday removed him from the field.

The first question one might well ask is, considering the basic premise of the Club, why a tournament anyway? Why this intrusion on the atmosphere of induced tranquility?

No man, dead or alive, has ever built a golf course that he didn't build hoping to challenge the best. Almost before Augusta National developed the first crown of grass on its acres, there arose among the guiding members a suggestion that the U.S. Open should be held there. Discussions even reached the level of the U.S. Golf Association, which supervises the Open, but there the project died. The sophisticated hybrid grasses that met U.S.G.A.'s rigid requirements in the

Jack Nicklaus pitching to 18th green after errant shot in 1974, the gallery providing background in its most colorful array.

southern summertime had not yet been developed, and there was no way the U.S.G.A. would consider moving the Open back to April. (As a matter of fact, until 1976 no U.S. Open had ever been played in a southern state, and only then in posthumous tribute to Bobby Jones in Atlanta.)

It was then in these early years that Clifford Roberts said, "Why don't we have our own tournament?" And they did. It is to be suspected that with Jones as the attraction and the new Club to be put on display, this idea had been carefully banked away in the back of his mind from the time he first laid eyes on "Fruitlands." But this suggested tournament did not come crashing out of the box as "great"; nor did it shoulder up to the U.S. Open and demand space at the top; nor did it announce to the world that here came the new member of the Big Four. Instead, it had to struggle to survive. Members had to get out of their Brooks Brothers clothes and sweat to make it work. The tournament had an arduous time before it earned its "Masters," in other words, due in one part to the fact that Jones and Roberts clung to their high ideals about how a golf tournament should be run.

In its first year, the Masters offered a total purse of $5,000, modest even in 1934, made up by donations of Club members. The gallery was excitingly and unexpectedly large, but Jones and Roberts operated by such non-compromising standards, bordering on extravagance, that the tournament suffered a substantial deficit. But the Masters was launched and there would be no turning back.

The Masters to this day is the only tournament of stature that gives away pairing sheets, spectator guides, parking, checkroom service, and observation seating — that's bleachers to racetracks and baseball parks — with the price of an admission ticket. Concession prices are considerably below those of other tournaments. The Club also absorbs the 3 percent state tax, and it is not to be overlooked that profits from such an event usually are taxed to about 50 percent by the Internal Revenue Service.

Whatever it may cost, the Masters maintains the most elaborate scoring system known to golf (and it originated most of it), such as the over (in green) and under (in red) hole-by-hole scores on the big boards. Not a piece of litter is allowed to survive any sundown on the Masters' grass. It was the first to uniform its caddies. It was the first to cover its course with a security force, the Pinkerton men — a great number of whom, by the way, are successful lawyers, dentists, doctors, and businessmen who take the week away from their offices and sign on to serve as their surest way of seeing the tournament. A spectator should never be surprised to find himself being directed about in the gallery by his own medical doctor.

A second barrier to the Masters becoming a "great" tournament was the very province with which Jones and Roberts had become enamored. When the tournament was a yearling, Augusta, as well as the surrounding area, was economically depressed, attractive as it was to golfing. Half the town was composed of people who could find no work and a class of population which wouldn't pay a dime to be chauffeured to see a man hit a golf ball. The "winter colony" had already gone home to its northern estates or was in the process of breaking up altogether. The military payroll had not yet grown to the point that it had by the 1960s, when Fort Gordon's was larger than that of all the industries of the city combined. That growth began with World War II. And when the impact did hit Augusta, it centered around the lower end of Broad Street, the main thoroughfare with all the cars parked in its middle,

44

and the naughty night joints and the tattoo parlors that entrapped eager, untraveled soldiers with sensuous desires and with pockets freshly lined with money. When daylight faded, lights on the marquees were turned up, sounds of instruments that grated elderly nerves gushed out into the night air, the go-go girls began their uncultured wiggling, and the soldiers piled off their buses and into action, leaving a wake of greenbacks. This was all as foreign to the Masters as miniature golf. There was no golfing clientele to be developed there.

Obviously, World War II had robbed the Masters of much of its momentum. The Club was closed shortly after the Masters of 1942 and was not reopened again until 1945, during which time some of the fairways had been turned into "victory gardens." Vegetables and farm produce were cultivated where Jones, Sarazen, Nelson, and Hogan had played their shots. When the members and the players returned, it had to be done all over again. Progress was slow. The public was finding other forms of entertainment. A new breed had been created by the war, men and women toughened by what they had experienced, calloused by battle and hardship, trying to pay themselves off for the thrills they'd missed.

As improbable as it may seem now, the Masters found itself financially unhealthy. It was forced to borrow from its members. The Augusta Merchants Association went about the city literally forcing blocs of tickets on member firms. Already a place of too few beds, too few restaurants, and too high prices during tournament week, a campaign was mounted to attack gouging, and the Chamber of Commerce organized a housing bureau in 1950 to accommodate guests who needed rooms at a reasonable rate. The word "hospitality" was attached to Masters week, and Augustans were encouraged to practice same. A Masters

ball and a Masters parade were added to the list of attractions, all of which have since faded from the scene, for they never really had a place in the mood of the Masters tournament.

Thus an interest had to be created beyond the area of Augusta, an appeal that would make this the one place in the world to be the first week in April. One of the gestures was to bring the Club membership out in full force during the tournament and insist upon an identity that would make them known to spectators in need of information. The green jacket was born out of the necessity of pressing Club members into service to keep down costs, which may come as crushing news to those who have thought it was created specifically to cloak the shoulders of the Olympians who won the Masters. "We bought these kelly green jackets in New York and asked all members to wear them," Clifford Roberts recalls. "If spectators wanted to know how to get to the 3rd green, a sandwich stand, or to a restroom, they could ask one of the men in the green jackets.

"It wasn't easy to convince some of our members that they should put on a coat that represented a uniform to them, like a maitre d', and stand around answering questions. They were reluctant at first. Now, the first thing they do when they get here is put on their green coats."

It wasn't until 1949 that the Masters champion was included among the exclusive green jacket wearers. Lloyd Mangrum, tied with Johnny Bulla as runner-up, held it while Sam Snead slipped into the first one awarded a winner. It became a Masters tradition, and today there's hardly a tournament played in the U.S. that the champion does not walk out with a blazer of some hue. But no one can see the green jacket except at the Masters for the Masters jacket is never allowed to be worn off the premises. Members have been expelled for such violation.

Of course the Masters champion also wins a check. A player gets $1,250 just for qualifying and showing up. Old-timers who don't strike a lick get $500 for appearing. But the champion also gets a. replica of the Masters Trophy to take home, a gold medal, and a silver box engraved with the signatures of all the contestants. En route to all this, it is also possible for him to win a pair of crystal goblets for eagles, a vase for a hole in one, and if you're wondering what Gene Sarazen got for his double eagle in 1935, it was a large Steuben crystal bowl, awarded retroactively in 1968.

In keeping with the traditions and the propriety of "auld gawfe," Augusta National still refers to its winner as "low professional," in deference to "low amateur." This has prompted such a jester as Lee Trevino, on the occasion of Gary Player's winning his second Masters, to refer to himself as "low Mexican."

Augusta, then, HAS become the one place in the world for a sportsman to be the first week in April. Seen by one player, Doug Sanders, it comes down to this: "If you don't get an invitation to the Masters, it's like being out of the world for a week."

What golf has done for Augusta has not been matched in any other community in the country, maybe the world, with the possible exception of St. Andrews. Augusta National IS the St. Andrews of America. The feeling is that if golf had been born on this side of the water and could have chosen its birthplace, Augusta National would have been it.

Of the foremost traditions of the Masters, one is a warm-up tournament played Wednesday afternoon on the Club's par-three course, which is laid out around Ike's Pond. Once a clinic occupied this position on the program, followed by a driving contest, but it was replaced several years ago, to the pleasure of all, by

this sylvan relaxation. The atmosphere is pure American picnic, though scores are kept and winners are awarded prizes. Players generally form their own pairings. Spectators can get close enough to their idols to chat with them, and even see the old champions, no longer participants in the Masters, play again. It takes on the character of a stroll through a living hall of fame.

Thursday morning on the 1st tee, yet another of the traditions is carried out for those who care to arise early enough to see the first players off. It has become ritual that Fred McLeod, who won the U.S. Open in 1908, and Jock Hutchison, who won the PGA championship in 1920 — the two oldest living winners of the two tournaments — deliver the first shots of the Masters. Until 1962 they played as regular invitees in the field, but McLeod had turned in the last 18-hole card of the two old-timers in 1958 when he played the course in 89 strokes at the age of 77.

They were appointed honorary starters in 1963, giving ground to the infirmities of age, and now they strike the first balls, set out down the 1st fairway, play two or three holes, then return to the clubhouse in carts. And another Masters is on, with a cast of thousands.

"Wear Your Badge, Please, Where It Can Be Seen."

Opposite page: Looking down upon the 6th green, with the dogwoods in splendid flower, from the hill where the tee is located.

Opposite page: Arnold
Palmer shooting for the 9th
green in 1974, divot flying.

Above: The 16th hole in
reverse, as it appears looking
back to the tee from the
green across the terrifying
stretch of water. Young Jim
Simons stands to the side as
veteran Herman Keiser
holes a putt.

Above: Pink dogwood on the 2nd hole, which bears
the name of the nearly 100 trees which flank it.

Left: The good Dr. Alister Mackenzie, kilts and
all, in his most widely circulated photograph.

The Course...Every Green a Stage

No. 7, the Pampas hole, looking down the narrow fairway to the bunkers
and small elevated green that require most delicate shot making.

"If the Masters had a rough, we wouldn't finish in two weeks."
— Lee Trevino

When the day is splashed with sunlight, and there is a touch of syrupy warmth in the air that plays on the horticultural outburst of Augusta National Golf Club grounds, there is no more beautiful place in American sport to be. Spring, it seems, has extracted every strain of color from the plants and shrubs and vines and trees. The green that covers its soil is so green it dazzles.

In this respect, golf has its edge over all the other games at which we spectate. Football rips its grass up in chunks. Horses run on drab, bare earth. Automobiles race on surfaces black with asphalt and stained with oil. Boats leave a wake of sludge on their waters. Baseball is played against a background of girders and concrete and an encirclement of seats for its jury. Basketball and hockey take to the grimness of warehouse life.

Golf wanders out among God's great outdoors, over hill and down into valley, through glen and glade. In no place has the natural beauty of the land been made so much a part of sport as here, where the Masters is played. There are greater golf courses. There are more spectacular golf courses. There are more excruciating tests of golf. There are other beautiful golf courses. But there is no great, spectacular, excruciating test of golf that is so beautiful as Augusta National. The key to it is that both the blossoming of spring and the arrival of the Masters coincide in all their natural and cultivated splendors.

The course on which the Masters is played today is only slightly akin to the "ideal golf course" on which Bobby Jones and Dr. Alister Mackenzie collaborated over 40 years ago. Only one tournament had been played before the most drastic of all changes was made. The nines were switched. The front nine became the back nine, and the back nine became the front nine. The hole on which the first field teed off in 1934 is now No. 10, measuring 410 yards then, measuring 485 yards now, one of the longest par fours in America, but favored by a 102-foot drop in elevation.

When it came time to plan the construction of the course, the choice of the architect was Jones' alone. Dr. Mackenzie was a Scot, and Jones had an affinity with Highland courses. He had seen the doctor's work and liked it and felt they could function comfortably together. Clifford Roberts had played and had high regard for courses Mackenzie had built in South America, if Jones' decision needed bolstering. Mackenzie's other greatest work in the U.S. is the Cypress Point course on Monterey Peninsula in California, where the Bing Crosby National Pro-Am is played.

Jones and Mackenzie had coinciding views on what constitutes the ideal golf course:

A really great golf course must be pleasurable to the greatest number possible.

It must require strategy as well as skill; otherwise it cannot be enduringly interesting.

It must give the average player a fair chance and at the same time require the utmost from the expert who tries for sub-par scores.

And, all natural beauty should be preserved, natural hazards should be utilized, and a minimum of artificiality introduced.

More succinctly, more deliciously phrased, Jones summed it up later in his book, *Golf Is My Game*, "We hope to make bogeys easy, if frankly sought, pars readily obtainable by standard good play,

and birdies, except on par-five holes, dearly bought."

Dr. Mackenzie — and what sort of doctor he was, we don't know — was as Scottish as a kilt, which, incidentally, he frequently wore, and his voice was heavy with the burr. It is a dreadful tragedy that the poor man never lived to see a round played on his masterpiece. Within a year after the completion of the course at Augusta National, he died in Scotland of unknown causes.

"A damned pity," Clifford Roberts said, "that he didn't have 10 more years left to spend in this country or we'd have had many more fine courses than we have."

Dr. Mackenzie departed this earth content with his handiwork. Before his death he pronounced Augusta National as "my best opportunity and, I believe, my finest achievement."

If there were any great emotional shocks over the reversal of the course in 1935, there is no record of them. In fact, it was years before late-arrivals on the scene of the Masters became aware that the order had ever been otherwise.

It is possible to gather a number of reasons for the change, depending on the company you keep. Byron Nelson speculates that it's because "the 10th hole is too tough for a starting hole, and it plays to a blind green. It's not a good starting point for spectators, either." Others surmise that it's because the present back nine tends to generate more drama, that it puts the finish on the proper stage. At least television can't be blamed, as it has been for nearly everything from the installation of the top 40-plus-10 cut of the field to soggy sandwiches. Television was 21 years in the future at the time.

Always in cases such as this, there's one authority to turn to. Clifford Roberts says the reason was as simple as this: "The [now] back nine is lower and more shaded, and gets the sun later in the day. The front nine is more suited to an early tee-off time than the old front nine."

Thus, the late Horton Smith holds one record that will never be challenged — that of playing the Masters in reverse in 284 strokes.

What has resulted are two different courses, or at least one with two distinctly different faces. The front nine is considerably less hazardous, yet not until the Saturday round of 1975, when Johnny Miller knuckled down to the occasion, had anyone ever played it in 30 strokes. As early as 1940, Jimmy Demaret had turned the back nine in 30.

There isn't a teapot of water to be found on the front nine, but the back nine is almost nothing but water from the 11th to the 17th hole. Five of those six holes lie there stealthily tempting, seducing, challenging the player to wet his feet. They were not meant to be courted for pars, but to induce either birdies or bogeys.

There is a harsh, distressing fact to be revealed beneath the surface of Augusta National. It has been acclaimed the piece of earth most perfectly fitted for a golf course by no other authority than Bobby Jones, but Augusta National would readily swap soil bases with Augusta Country Club, just over the fence from the 12th green, or with the Forest Hills course, just a short drive across town, and now the property of Fort Gordon. Both are sand-based. Augusta National's base is pure clay.

"It's great for growing pine trees," Clifford Roberts said, "but it collects and holds water. After a while it springs a leak, and these leaks become bogs around the fairways and the greens. Usually, we'll have to repair 10 to 12 of these leaks each year, tile them, and drain them off."

Early in the construction stage of the course, there was conjecture that Jones and Mackenzie intended to recreate some of the great holes of the great courses Jones had played in competition. Both of them disavowed this, and Jones later reaffirmed the disavowal, pointing out that such a project would have been rather presumptuous. However, as Mackenzie wrote his own impressions of the course, hole by hole, he was not able to refrain from reference to other holes of other outstanding courses of the world.

The 4th hole struck him as similar to the 17th, or Road hole at St. Andrews. The 5th had characteristics of the Redan hole at North Berwick. The 6th hole reminded him of the 11th, or the famous Eden hole at St. Andrews. There was a trace of the 18th at St. Andrews in the 7th hole. The 8th hole, before all the mounds were removed in 1956, could be compared to the 17th at Muirfield. The 10th hole "embodies the most attractive features of the 13th at Cypress Point," he said. The 12th hole, the short par three across Rae's Creek, has some of the devil of the 17th at Cypress Point in it. The 16th hole, the par three across the pond, was not unlike the best hole at Stoke Poges in England in its original state, when the only water was a small stream. And the 17th hole reminded him of No. 14 at St. Andrews.

The strong influence of St. Andrews, where Jones won the British Amateur, is not difficult to detect; but a great number of those features have long since disappeared, to the point that Augusta National now is a unique personality, and some of its holes have become models for reproductions on other courses around the world.

Each of the holes bears a name of affection, not so much as pets as in relation to the foliage thereabouts. And in order:

No. 1, Tea Olive — 400 yards, par four, slight dogleg right around outreaching pines, a favorable starting hole which has been eagled four times, first by Frank Moore of Texas in 1940, Roberto de Vicenzo as he began that fateful Sunday round of his in 1968, Takaaki Kono, a smallish Japanese pro, in 1970, and Lou Graham in 1976.

No. 2, Pink Dogwood — 555 yards out of a chute that opens up on a large bunker to the right at the top of a hill that slants left and downward toward a broad green guarded by two bunkers. Not the most frequently birdied par five on the course.

No. 3, Flowering Peach — 360 yards, par four, inviting forest trouble on the right, green on a plateau, narrow and difficult to hold.

No. 4, Flowering Crabapple — 220 yards, next to No. 12 the most difficult par three. Approached over a yawning trap guarding an evil green of exasperating undulations.

No. 5, Magnolia — 450 yards, par four, recommended tee shot landing area is the elevation to the right. Fairway bunker on the left, but only one around the green, and that to the rear, whose angles and inclines and swales can give a putter a severe case of the jimjams. Art Wall eagled it in 1974.

No. 6, Juniper — 190 yards, par three, elevated tee overlooking a good-sized green, gets more birdie play than any of the short holes. It was here that Billy Joe Patton dropped his electrifying ace in 1954, the shot traveling over crowds of people scrambling down the path below him.

No. 7, Pampas — 365 yards, par four, most deceiving measurements. Sounds simple, but tee shot demands position, and the approach must be as delicate as surgery. Three bunkers guard the entry to an elevated green that is neither deep nor wide, and two more lurk behind the green.

No. 8, Yellow Jasmine — 530 yards, par five, tee adjoining the 7th, 2nd, and 17th

greens and the 3rd tee at one of the focal spectator points on the course. It's a long, hard climb up a hill that flattens out to the left where the green is located. A three-shot approach, but Bruce Devlin made it to the cup in two in 1967, only the second double eagle in a Masters.

No. 9, Carolina Cherry — 440 yards, par four, and they keep stretching it out. Woods to the left, woods to the right, huge landing area opening to the foot of a hill. Treacherous putting anywhere from above the pin.

No. 10, Camellia — 485 yards, par four, but a drop of 102 feet from tee to green. It was 10 yards longer than No. 13 until the par-five hole was extended in 1975. A dramatically beautiful fairway that sweeps down the hill into a hollow with a backdrop of stately old pines.

No. 11, White Dogwood; No. 12, Golden Bell; and No. 13, Azalea — the "Amen Corner."

No. 14, Chinese Fir — 420 yards, par four, fairway guarded to the left by over-hanging trees and slanting to the right. Another of those suicidal greens as at No. 5. Like Nos. 5, 7, 11, and 18, it never loses any shots to the field. Allen Miller eliminated the bother of a putt in 1975. He sank his approach from about 160 yards out, the only eagle here in 39 years.

No. 15, Fire Thorn — 520 yards, par five, sometimes the easiest, sometimes the most devastating of the par fives, depending on the tempting or non-tempting vagaries of the weather. Not one of the players' favorites because of the mountain of a mound erected on the right of the fairway in the old landing area. The lake in front of the green has caught many a leader's hopes, and others have gone for it depending on the spectators circling the area, or the bunker on the right, to back-stop shots too strong or off line. Never to be overlooked as the site of Gene Sarazen's double eagle that tied Craig Wood in 1935.

No. 16, Redbud — 190 yards, par three, all carry over a dyed pond. Described by Jack Nicklaus as "the most exciting scene in tournament golf." Also, where he sank his "most exciting putt" of 40 feet that turned him in the right direction on the way home to his victory in 1975.

No. 17, Nandina — 400 yards, par four, catches the brunt of many a charge of some fellow in a hurry to fetch a green jacket, as it did Art Wall in 1959, Arnold Palmer in 1962, and Gary Player in 1974. Large tree guards the fairway's right side. Another green full of devilish tricks and hard to hold.

No. 18, Holly — 420 yards, par four, probably has seen more dramatics and hysterics than any golf hole in America. Tee shots rocket out between two clumps of trees to a ridge that crosses at the landing area. Bunker and a crop of sapling trees to the left. Bunkered to the right and left, the green is long and narrow and slick as linoleum. Doug Ford birdied out of the trap and won it here in 1957. Palmer won it here in 1960 and lost it in 1961 and tied it in 1962. And Hogan and Ford and Fred Hawkins and Bobby Nichols and Johnny Miller and Tom Weiskopf and others too numerous to name have missed the putt here that would have given them a second chance.

All told, 3,510 yards long on the front nine, 3,520 yards on the back side, coming to 7,030 yards with a conservative number of 42 bunkers and approximately 100,000 square feet of putting green.

Some love it, some hate it. Jimmy Demaret said one year, after a particularly distressing round, "They ought to plow it up and start all over again." Gene Sarazen said, "It wasn't much the first time I saw it. I was disappointed. I'd expected much more. I never was an admirer of Mackenzie's golf courses, anyway. The alterations and the improvements have made it a great course now." Jack Nicklaus said,

"What has happened here is what made it great."

It's a course for shotmakers, free of gimmicks and the pastures called "rough" of the U.S. Open. There is no rough here. Trees, water, and sand, but no rough. "If Augusta National had a rough," Lee Trevino has said, "we wouldn't finish in two weeks."

The proof of the Masters' stature is found in the fabric of its champions. Multiple winners, those who have won it twice or more each, represent a sort of roundup of classic names in golf. Among them, Nicklaus, Palmer, Demaret, Snead, Hogan, Nelson, Smith, and Player accumulated 23 championships. Each name is found among the winners of at least one of the three major professional tournaments, except Smith and Demaret, and they were Ryder Cup team members, leading money winners, and Demaret took home the Vardon Trophy one year.

Of the remaining 16 champions, half were winners of at least one of the other three big ones — the U.S. Open, the British Open, or the PGA championship. Among those who were not, Art Wall won the Tournament of Champions and the Canadian Open; Gay Brewer won the Canadian Open and Japanese Masters; Tommy Aaron won the Canadian Open; and Bob Goalby had a record of 11 tournament successes. Charles Coody, George Archer, and Herman Keiser kept winning to a minimum, and Claude Harmon kept it out of sight. The Masters was the only tournament he ever won.

Arnold Palmer and caddy doing a dance and exercising some body English trying to help a putt find the cup on the 13th green.

Above: Johnny Miller chipping to the 13th green as Dave Stockton, former PGA champion, watches in a scene from 1973.

Left: Bruce Devlin stroking a fairway shot on the 11th hole, scene of the Australian's disastrous 8 in 1968.

"Where more Masters are lost" — the 12th, probably the world's most notorious par-three hole, as it appears from green to tee. Hogan's Bridge to the right, 13th fairway to the left.

The 11th green, viewed across the pond that guards the approach, here, due to the perspective, looking like a crater filled with water.

Amen Corner...the Critical Triangle

Jack Nicklaus putts, Gay Brewer and Tommy Jacobs watch as the three play the 13th hole on Monday after their 72-hole tie in 1966.
Winning the play-off, Nicklaus became the first successful defending champion.

"It invites . . . an eagle, a birdie, a par, or any catastrophe he brings upon himself."

Amen Corner — the name comes from the strong Protestant influence that belts the South. What basis there is for linkage eludes most of us, for the Fundamentalist preacher has always considered the game of golf an unworthy challenger to his Sunday priority, a frivolous distraction that takes his men from their proper places in family pews to the weekly dogfight and accompanying evils of the men's grill at the Country Club.

Amen Corner at Augusta National refers to a stretch of three holes that bluntly introduces the player to the seriousness of the outgoing nine. Its disposition is revealed to the Masters in satanic form. It cuts down, it beguiles, it ensnares; it has wiped out the dream of many a leader who came marching into this intersection of the 11th, 12th, and 13th holes with devastation on his mind and made the turn back toward the club-house as the devastated. Every noble golf course has its point of crisis, real or imagined. Perhaps no more tournaments are won or lost in this area than any other, but the vision is in the eyes of the beholder. So magnetic is the challenge of Amen Corner that the eyes pop out here in glorious awe; thus this is the loca-tion that attracts the largest galleries of the tournament until the final twosome of players approaches the 18th hole on Sunday.

Spectators have multiple choices of action — the drives on the 11th, as the balls come bounding down the fairway out of the chute in the pines where the tee is located; the approaches and action on that green; the full play of the 12th; and the drives around the elbow of the

61

13th hole. Mainly, the gallery takes its station at a point that reaches out between the 12th tee and the 13th fairway where it takes its turn left and into the glen. The 13th green finds refuge among the flowering azaleas and the shadowing pines.

Strictly for descriptive purposes, arithmetic is wasted on even the average golf course. It's like trying to analyze a ravishing beauty simply by reciting her bust, waist, and hip measurements. Thus, the 11th hole is not simply 445 yards of Richmond County designed to be played in four strokes. The broad fairway tapers down to an approach severely constricted on the left by a pond that seems magnetized and then rushes off a series of mounds to flatten out into the green that fits like a foot to a leg.

In numbers, the 12th hole sounds tame as a tabby cat. Simply, 155 yards, par three. Actually viewed, it is something sinister. The line of flight from tee to green takes a slanting course across Rae's Creek — ah, Rae's Creek, we shall hear more of it — to a slender green that runs parallel to the water and perpendicular to the tee, guarded by one bunker between creek and green, and backed up by a pair of bunkers cut out of the sharply rising bank beyond. Rae's Creek is a seemingly disinterested little ribbon of water that cuts through this sector of the back nine (the Augusta Country Club course is just over the fence back of the 12th green) whose impact on American golf has been monumental. The Mississippi River is longer and wider and more historic, but Rae's Creek is just as wet and twice as treacherous in its own way. The story of its life can be told by the number of golf balls it has swallowed up in the tension of classic competition.

The 12th green and 13th tee sit across Rae's Creek on what appear to be little stages of their own. Only officials cross what has been known as "Hogan's Bridge" since its dedication in 1958. No gallery has ever shared that portion of Augusta National except as one shares theater. Drives on the 13th hole whistle out across Rae's Creek into a sharp "hook" turn along a tilted fairway. Here again, figures are deceivers. "A tempting and dangerous hole," Bobby Jones called it. Another of those Loreleis that invites a bold player to disaster, and yet, as par fives go, it generously carries out the Jones concept most sportingly. He looked with annoyance upon par-five holes on which "you don't start playing golf until your third shot." No. 13 is only 485 yards long. But devilishly deceiving because of the hazards of attempting the hook around the dogleg, and a little brook that trickles unconsciously along fronting the green like Nature's appointed guardian.

Some journalists have referred to the 13th as the "key hole of the Masters." It taunts the player to get home in two strokes. It invites him to have his chance at an eagle, a birdie, a par, or any catastrophe he brings upon himself. More often than not, it's a friend to the gambling attacker and has created more kings than commoners. Take 1974, for instance, when the 13th hole was played in 67 strokes under par by the whole field, easiest mark of the tournament.

This critical triangle of holes began reaching out for a special identity as early as the fourth year of the Masters. Ralph Guldahl, a slope-shouldered hulk of a man, then playing out of Dallas, Texas, was at the top of his cyclical career. He would win the U.S. Open twice in a row, the Western Open three times, and, eventually, the Masters. In this year, 1937, he approached the 12th hole four strokes in the lead and cruising. He took the precarious route from tee to pin, requiring utmost precision en route to this narrow patch of green, and his shot fell into Rae's Creek. On the 13th hole, his approach found the trickle of a stream in front of the green. When he was through, Guldahl had used 11 strokes to play two holes designed to be played in 8.

Right behind him came Byron Nelson, flapping along in the balloon-legged, pleated trousers of the time, as yet a young man in the clutches of unrelenting obscurity. He was a former railway clerk who had never won more than a sectional tournament. Nelson also took the precarious route on the 12th, but he made it and sank his putt for a birdie.

His long approach shot found the green on the 13th and came to rest eight feet from the pin. He eagled to go with his birdie on the 12th. He had played the two holes in five strokes, three below par, six below Guldahl. Nelson picked up the lead and bore it home to the clubhouse as nerveless as an experienced winner.

Just as cruelly as the tournament had been snatched from Guldahl's faltering grip by these holes in 1937, it was on them that he staked out his claim to the championship two years later. A spoon delivered his second shot 230 yards and six feet from the pin on the 13th. With his eagle, he shut the door on Sam Snead, not one to be pitied as the coming years would reveal.

Little Thomas Aaron, wistful of face and aged 13, sat on the front seat of the family car and rode from Gainesville to Augusta on Easter Sunday of 1950, there to see for himself the first time this great golf tournament. His father, who drove, had spoken of it many times. His father is a golf professional, one who runs small clubs and keeps the greens and realizes that it will never be otherwise with him.

Later, when Tommy Aaron, then aged 36, still somewhat wistful in a middle-aged sort of way, won the Masters for himself, he thought back upon the first time he had seen this course. Details had escaped his mind, but his remembering took a peculiar form of the empathetic. "Jim Ferrier almost had it won," he said, being one who also had many tournaments 'almost won,' "and then he started bogeying on the way in and somebody else won. I can't remember who, but I remember feeling sorry, so sorry for Ferrier."

Jimmy Demaret had won it, not one to be overwhelmed by vagueness, with his splendorous wardrobe of flashing color and his tassled haberdashery. More than that, Demaret had won the Masters twice before. But Tommy Aaron's memory honored the one who lost it, for his sympathy lay with him.

The axis of the tournament had been this theatrical 13th hole once more. Demaret had played it in 4-3-3-4, or six under par, five strokes less than Ferrier, who lost the lead and the green coat that would never be his, by a margin of two strokes.

Down from the hills of North Carolina they came whooping and yowling in 1954, yanked away from the weekend dogfights at their own modest courses by the exciting bulletins out of Augusta, Georgia, about one of their own kind. Billy Joe Patton of the Mimosa Golf Club in Morganton, North Carolina, would not have been in the field for the Masters of 1954 had not Clifford Roberts asked Bobby Jones, as they pondered their list, "Shouldn't the alternates be invited along with the regular members of the Walker Cup team?"

Billy Joe was an alternate and invited. By Sunday, he had assaulted the very dignity of the Masters, stormed about the course like some weekend player having the kind of hot streak reserved only for wild revelries, and had Sam Snead and Ben Hogan on the run. When his kith and kin infiltrated the galleries for the weekend, the sounds that arose took on a rodeo quality. The grandest shout of them all arose Sunday when his tee shot found the cup for an ace on the 6th, and he took the lead. Thus, Patton, walking with the stride of a plowman, surged into the 13th hole, his Tar Heel clan loping along behind him. When he made the bold attempt, the only kind he knew, and went for the green after a feckless tee shot, the ball found the edge of the ditch. Barefoot, he started in after it, reassessed his position, took a penalty, and chipped across. By the time the ball found the cup, Billy Joe Patton had used seven strokes, lost the lead, and had not become the first amateur to win the Masters. The next day Snead beat Hogan by a stroke for the championship, but 1954 is marked in memory as the year the aweless mountaineer Patton almost did it for all amateurs everywhere.

"Cut down by Amen Corner," he chirped, mirthful in the face of disappointment, "but we gave 'em a few thrills, didn't we!"

When Arnold Palmer first began to acknowledge Augusta National as the mother of his destiny, he found himself strongly in the favor of Amen Corner. It supplied the root for his emergence and for the craze that swept through golf in his name. But not too swiftly here, for there is perspective to be established.

We must retreat into the Eisenhower years. It was 1958. Mark McCormack had not yet graduated from Yale School of Law to become his agent. Thus, Palmer had not yet endorsed his first Mercury, the automobile; his first L & M, the cigaret; nor had he developed affiliation with the umbrella that was to become the symbol of everything he touched. He was no more a name than Dow Finsterwald, who would win the PGA championship, or Bill Casper, who would win the U.S. Open, or Mike Souchak, big and amiable and seemingly capable of winning anything anytime he tamed his putter. Palmer had won seven tournaments, but they were swallowed up and digested by time,

such is the durability of the tradition of the Insurance City Open, the Eastern Open, the Rubber City Open, and others that pass in the night. There was one hint of what was to come — a few days before, he had won the St. Petersburg Open.

On Sunday morning, April 6, 1958, Palmer was noticed checking out of the Richmond Hotel, then the most desirable public address in Augusta. "Either," said one observant spectator, "a brazen show of confidence, or a wretched show of faintheartedness."

Which of these it was, the spectator was never to know, but it is now history that on that fourth day Palmer started, tied for the lead with Sam Snead at 211, and at the end of the day emerged the winner. But not without being the center of a drama played out on the 12th hole at which point Ken Venturi, his playing partner on Sunday, had come within one stroke of the lead. Palmer's tee shot became imbedded back of the green in a spongy bank; he was forced to play the imbedded ball at the insistence of an official and holed out with a 5. Invoking a rule of the day, he then dropped a second ball and played it as a provisional for a par 3. At this point, Palmer was either leading Venturi and the entire tournament by a stroke with his 3, or he was trailing Venturi by a stroke with his 5. It was not until Palmer and Venturi reached the 14th hole that the ruling was made. The 3 was cleared as the official score and four holes later Palmer claimed his first Masters victory.

It could not be felt on the wind or read in the muddy inscriptions left by his spikes, but Palmer was keeping a date with the inevitable. Once more, Amen Corner had dictated the plot and Palmer had played to it, though by no means could his round that Sunday have been considered one of the "charges" with which his name was to become synonymous. His final round was played in 73 strokes.

The fact is, he was overwhelmed by the "charge" of a man his distinct opposite the following year. Once more, we pick up our hero as he approached the 12th hole in the lead. He drew his weapon from its sheath, a seven-iron, and he aimed his shot toward the green. A gasp raced through the gallery on the point. The ball had plopped into the water of the creek. Palmer dropped, absorbing a one-stroke penalty, and his next shot missed the green! By the time he was through, he had required six strokes on the hole, a triple bogey. He was out of it.

Art Wall, thin, slightly slouched and deaconlike, swirled by Palmer with uncharacteristic ebullience and bravado. He birdied five of the last six holes, never done before, and he won the Masters of 1959, one stroke over Cary Middlecoff, two over Palmer. Once more . . . once more, in all its unauthorized austerity, Amen Corner handed down another deadly decision.

Friday is not so dramatic a point. It is only the day of the second round of the four. But in 1968 there was a certain rarity about the scoring of Bruce Devlin, an Australian who later became Americanized, that commanded particular study. He was sacked by one hole on Amen Corner, his one lapse in four days. No. 11 took its turn at cussedness. Each of the other three days, Devlin responded with a dogged consistency and shot 69s.

As he played the 11th in the Friday round, he brought a two-stroke lead to the hole. The hole being a par four, and guarded on its left by a pond, the player's inclination is to "leave" his approach iron out to the right and "draw" the ball back to come into the green from the non-dunkable side. Unfortunately, Devlin "drew" his second shot too sharply and the ball found the water. He dropped. His fourth shot fell short and almost rolled back into the pond. He took a one-sided stance on the bank and struck viciously at the ball — and missed it. In the process, the ball had become a bit more exposed, and now he finally removed himself from his horrid plight with a shot that reached the green. But he three-putted—for an 8!

Without the quadruple bogey, he would have had another 69. Also, he would have won the tournament by a stroke. But this disconsolate experience of making an 8 did not dampen his Aussie courage. He was still in the chase coming down to the back nine on Sunday, the day it became a race of Bob Goalby, Roberto de Vicenzo, and an errant pencil. Goalby won it clean and clear when the Argentine signed an incorrect scorecard.

"It did not bother me," Devlin said, still somewhat hollowly, of his downfall at the 11th, "until the tournament was over and I had lost by three strokes. A par wins it. Even a bogey ties for it. That's when it got to me. I could have cried. I could have cursed. Instead, I sagged all over."

Thus, we take our leave of Amen Corner—the champions and the losers it has created, and those yet to come who will find a crisis there. We leave them all to heaven.

Craig Wood putting out on the 18th green in 1941, an old and oft denied challenger finally rewarded with a Masters championship.

Above: This immortal foursome pauses in practice round of 1935: (L-R) Gene Sarazen, Bobby Jones, Walter Hagen, and Tommy Armour.

Left: Lloyd Mangrum, who held the course record of 64 for 25 years, strikes a movie idol pose as he lights up.

Bobby Jones putting on the 2nd green on a cold day in April, accompanied by Horton Smith.

Now on the First Tee...Ralph Stonehouse

Ralph Stonehouse, who struck the first shot of the Masters
in 1934, in his playing prime.

"... And the Masters was launched with modest aspirations...."

The year was 1934. One year into the New Deal, the NRA, and Franklin Delano Roosevelt's residency in the White House. The Charleston Open tournament had been played the week before in coastal South Carolina, among the oaks with moss dripping from their limbs like hair. Paul Runyan, a wee fellow not many years removed from a farm in Arkansas, had won it. Now the players moved swiftly for their cars, and over the two-lane blacktop highways aimed themselves in the direction of Augusta in their Ford V-8s, their Desotos, their LaSalles, and their Packards.

Also, up from Florida they came, the professionals from the North who wintered in the South like the birds. They were on their way back to their home courses, thawing out now as winter gave way to spring, and March moved nearer April. This year there was something to break the trip. For the fortunate, there was an invitation to play a tournament on this grand new course that Bobby Jones and Dr. Alister Mackenzie had built in the Grand Slammer's name and which was supported by his friends and admirers and was called Augusta National Golf Club. Even some players who didn't have invitations were stopping off, attracted to the scene by the glow of this man, caught up in his mystique. America would be able to see him play in competition again for the first time in four years, since he had completed the Feat Impossible — winning the U.S. Open, the U.S. Amateur, the British Open, and the British Amateur all in the same year. Golfing professionals stood almost as much in awe of the occasion as the public. Curiosity besieged them. The

Second Coming, as it were.

Calcutta pools were as prominent as buck teeth in those times. This is the auction in which players' names are sold to the highest bidder, who collects a share of the pot proportionate to the finish of his man if he's among the leaders. With sentiment rampant over logic, Jones brought the highest bid, $680, in the ballroom of the Bon Air Vanderbilt. Runyan was second — $550. They would be paired for the first round the next day.

Not even the results of an informal little two-ball tournament over the course that afternoon had discouraged Jones' buyer. The host and Ross Somerville, the best of Canada's amateurs, could only score a 76 on their best ball, four over par.

Nowhere in the accountings and the conversation or in the Calcutta bidding did the name Ralph Stonehouse assume any degree of prominence. He was one of the professionals from the colder climes working his way North from Florida to the Charles H. Coffin Municipal Club in Indianapolis. He was coming from his most shining hour. His only shining hour as a tournament tour player, as it would turn out. Ralph Stonehouse had won the first tournament of the year, the Miami Open, thus accounting for an invitation from this man he knew only as one who had consented to come down from Olympus. Stonehouse did not enjoy fame then, nor did he ever.

He was a smallish young man, fragile as a leaf and as brisk in manner as the winds of that month. He wore slicked-down black hair and ran to sweaters in dress, complete in the haberdashery of the golfing time to the white shirt and necktie, for men did dress for the course in that era as if they had only moments before left an important conference at the office. With his pug little nose and his flashing smile Ralph Stonehouse might have been lifted directly from the film can of a Johnny Downs movie with Priscilla Lane.

Only in retrospect does he emerge here an actor of significance in the continuing drama of the tournament then known as Augusta National Invitational, and merely for timing alone. He appeared briefly on stage as a major figure, then just as swiftly dissolved into the oblivion of sport. Perhaps because he had won the first tournament of the professional tour that year was he thus honored to be first off the tee on the first round of the first Masters-to-be on this March 22, 1934.

The day broke bright and clear, with a touch of an invigorating chill in the air. The new course, in its coat of winter rye, rolled out down the hill from the old manor house, greener than Scotland itself. "What a sad thing it is," said a man named George Jacobus, then president of the professional golfers organization, "that the good Dr. Mackenzie, with all his kindliness, did not live to see it as the thing of beauty it is today."

Precisely at 9:45 in the morning, Ralph Stonehouse stepped out into the sunshine of the 1st tee, delivered his driver into the pegged ball, struck it down the fairway, and the Masters was launched with modest aspirations to assume in time a stature that would have stunned the most perceptive one among those of golfing vision gathered there. Stonehouse hit a five-iron to the green, used two putts for par, and was on his way to finish even with Leo Diegel in sixteenth place. This entitled him to a renewal of his invitation, but falling out of the leading 24 the next year, he lost his place and retains a hairbreadth hold in the legend of golf only as the man who hit the first shot in the Masters.

. . . Rediscovered on Sixth Street

U.S. 441 roars through south Florida as it gets a running start for the Great

Smokies. It roars because it is a four-lane national highway and automobiles roar. In this heavy end of Florida, overloaded with people, every passageway not posted or under construction seethes with vehicles going to or coming from somewhere, especially in "the season."

Plantation is a suburb of Ft. Lauderdale, as Ardmore is of Philadelphia, or as Cicero is of Chicago. There's no boundary visible to the naked eye. Sixth Street is an asphalt tributary of 441, and you turn at Dan Dowd's restaurant. The little thoroughfare is as unpretentious as its name, quiet and typically "retirement" Florida. It dead-ends into Ft. Lauderdale Country Club, but about "a four-wood shot," in the phrasing of Ralph Stonehouse, before reaching the club gate, you come upon his name on a mailbox. This has been Ralph Stonehouse's home for about 10 years, or since he sold out the club in Lockport, New York, and came South, following the "snowbird" trail to the land of promised sunshine. A late-model Cadillac is at anchor in the garage. Out of sight all these years, Ralph Stonehouse has prospered obviously.

Mrs. Stonehouse answers the bell and leads you into a huge room built for relaxing. A little man with a somewhat pinched face and a small snub nose issues a greeting. He wears a beige sweater and a chartreuse turtleneck shirt. His hair is no longer slicked back but hangs loosely below the nape of the neck, like that of an old film character actor. Wallace Ford, for instance.

It has been 73 years since he was delivered upon this earth in Scott County, Indiana, but rare is the day that passes that he isn't seen moving out of his driveway in his electric golf cart, humming down Sixth Street to Ft. Lauderdale Country Club. He plays regularly and has cards of rounds in the low 70s to show for it. He displays them as proudly as a boy showing off a good report card, but since his operation he is seldom able to hit a drive more than 150 yards.

He is watching a football game between the Miami Dolphins and Houston Oilers but turns his back on it to be hospitable. "If I watch them, something always goes wrong, anyway," he says. Nevertheless, the television blares on, Mrs. Stonehouse excuses herself to back the Cadillac out of the garage and go to the grocery, and to the background of occasional yips of a dachshund named Heinie, Ralph Stonehouse talks with the animation of a man delighted that the world has discovered him again.

"I got one of the first invites," he says. His delivery is rapid and his volume just above a whisper. "Very formal. It had an RSVP at the bottom. Everybody called it simply 'Bobby Jones' tournament.'

"There were about 60 of us, I think. Some were personal friends of Bobby's, but most of them had won tournaments or were outstanding golfers of the time. I had won the Miami Open in January, the first tournament of the year. I beat an old Scottish pro, Willie Dow, in a play-off at the Biltmore course. Willie came from Scotland, but he was a pro then at some club in Wisconsin where it was as cold as a pawnbroker's heart."

Stonehouse had left his shop at the Charles H. Coffin course in Indianapolis to play what the winter professional tour consisted of in those times: first, a dreadful drive to California, then back across the continent, sometimes breaking the trip with a tournament in El Paso or San Antonio.

"Sometimes we played on 'greens' of oiled sand, and one time in El Paso they were made out of pressed cottonseed. Fellow named Guy Paulsen from Ft. Wayne set a record on those things that nobody's ever gonna break. He played a round with 18 putts. Three of us traveled together in those times. Tony Manero

71

traveled with me some. You know, he won the Open in '36 at Baltusrol. Owns a restaurant down here at Hallandale now. The big pros usually stayed in hotels. Three of us got a room for $7 a week. We didn't live in luxury like these boys today. We played tournaments in everything but gravel pits, and we slept anyplace we could get a rate and a pillow."

When he arrived in Augusta for the first Masters, Stonehouse was one of the club professionals who had made the drive from Florida, homing in on their shops in the North like pigeons returning to their lofts.

"There were two carloads of us. I had the only invite. When we checked in at the Richmond Hotel in Augusta, they put us all in a salesman's display room on the fifth floor."

Enriched by his victory in Florida and feeling an obligation to live less gypsy-like since he was arriving as a guest of the great Bobby Jones, he had felt affluent enough to seek out a hotel instead of a rooming house. Stonehouse shared his display room at the Richmond with another pro from Rochester, New York, a golf ball salesman, and a one-armed pro from Texas. They'd come to watch.

"I don't know why I was picked to be the first one off. Maybe it was because I'd won the first tournament. If I do say it myself, I was considered one of the better short players back then. I only weighed 132 pounds. I had to be good with my irons.

"That reminds me, I ought to correct something. I've read somewhere that Johnny Kinder was paired with me, but he wasn't. I teed off first and Jim Foulis, Jr., teed off behind me. He was a pro at some club in Chicago. We were paired together the first two rounds. I hit a good drive and a five-iron and got a 4. The green was L-shaped and the pin was just around the corner in the L. It sat down in

a little swale right at the bottom of the hill. You see, the nines were reversed the next year. That hole is now the 10th.

"The second day the weather wasn't very good. Starting times were switched, and Jim and I teed off last. The third day I was paired with Johnny Dawson, one of the top amateurs. The weather turned cold, and we played in a light drizzle."

It was at this point that the drop on the thermometer was accompanied by a rise in our man Stonehouse's score. It is good to point out, however, that the honor of leading the way had not been squandered on a player who had not responded with golfing eloquence. After two rounds Stonehouse was locked in a tie for third with MacDonald Smith and Jimmy Hines at 144 strokes. Horton Smith, who would win it, was only two strokes ahead. Bobby Jones was six strokes further back. Still, the headlines of Atlanta papers ran to The Master himself, for the city sat and waited breathlessly for news of its hero's return to his game.

The Masters was front-page copy in Atlanta newspapers as it began ("Masters" had not become official, except in the judiciary of sports departments), but by the end of the tournament the story had been moved inside. Jones was not winning. Anticipation had lost its edge after his round of 76 the first day. Atlanta had conceded that its pipe dream was indeed just that, a pipe dream. Its Prince Valiant would not return to the wars a champion. Meanwhile, Ralph Stonehouse was referred to briefly as "youthful Miami Open champion," after which the writer fled on.

"I was out in 31 in my second round, and it was years before that record was tied. I was very much in contention the first two rounds, but the weather turned and I finished 75-76, 11 strokes behind Horton Smith. He won it with 284.

"While I was very serious, dedicated to making a good showing, I still remember

Bobby Jones and Gene Sarazen, one of his closest friends among the professionals of the time, enjoy the shade of the spreading oak on the terrace lawn.

the atmosphere as very informal. Some of the fellows made a big party out of it. There was nothing like the pressure there is at the Masters today. I played just two years, and I haven't been back since. I ought to go back one of these days. I do remember making the remark to some of the fellows, 'One day all the players in the world are going to want to get an invite to this tournament.'

"I was reading some place awhile ago about Gary Player walking down the fairway with another player who mentioned the fellow who hit the first shot at the Masters. Player asked, 'What's his name?'

"' Ralph Stonehouse,' the other fellow said.

"'That's a man I must meet,' Player said.

'That's almost as good as winning it.'"

Nearly a million shots have been hit since in the Masters. Some have decided who won and who didn't. Some have flown straight from the tee to the cup. Aces. Some have risen from the fairway and found the cup. Eagles. Some have found the water and some have found the sand. But none can hold the significance of Ralph Stonehouse's. None can ever be first again.

Goodbyes are said at the door. The Dolphins and the Oilers are still wrestling in colorful agony on the television screen. Only when the radio comes on in the rented car does it come to light that Ralph Stonehouse's scheme of inattention has not worked. The Dolphins have been startlingly beaten. Upset.

Gene Sarazen...Chief Double Eagle

Gene Sarazen and his friend Vic Ghezzi, former PGA champion, stride across one of Augusta National's hillocks.

"What made the Masters the Masters?"

"Bob Jones, of course. His presence. Then the double eagle."

— Clifford Roberts

No such monumental shot of golf has ever been struck on this earth. Never ever.

Even to this day, four decades later, merely the mention of "double eagle" dredges it to the surface out of a past so ancient it seems disconnected from now. No further identification is required. It is as if it were the only double eagle ever scored in a golf tournament, and Gene Sarazen reached into his bag and pulled it out from among his tricks of the game when he found himself sorely in need.

Yet, it is not even the only double eagle ever made in a Masters. There has been one other, the only other as we stand time still for this moment. From down the hill, around a gentle dogleg, out of sight of the 8th green, Bruce Devlin, an Australian, delivered a four-wood shot from the fairway that found the cup and accumulated for himself the equivalent of three birdies with one swing in the first round of 1967. But it was a shot of no consequence. Without it, Devlin would have wound up with 77 strokes instead of 74.

It was the circumstance that stood Gene Sarazen in such good stead with immortality. It was more than the perfect wedding of club face and ball; it was the whole tournament. The Masters of 1935.

First, though, let us take up some rein and back up in time to get a clear focus on the Gene Sarazen (né Eugene Saraceni) of those years and how he stood on the ladder of the game. He was, indeed, the dominant professional golfer of that era, no less a Palmer or a Nicklaus of the roiling '30s than Palmer or Nicklaus is the Sarazen of the '60s and '70s. It behooves us, as a matter of fact, to have a closer look at just what items are entered into the record beside the name of Gene Sarazen, son of an immigrant Italian carpenter.

—Youngest winner of the U.S. Open in 1922 at the age of 20, a victory he repeated in 1932, the same year he won the British Open and also celebrated becoming the first golfer to be named Associated Press Athlete of the year.

—Three-time winner of the PGA championship, 1922, 1923, 1933. (Note the 10-year span again.)

—First winner of all the four major professional golf championships of the world, the U.S. and British Opens, the PGA championship, and the Masters, which this double eagle was about to unlock for him and thereby implant his name forevermore on the mosaic of Augusta National.

Sarazen was making $20,000 a year when it was unheard of in golf and seemingly unreachable by any other mortal using these complex tools of the trade. So paramount a figure was he that a man named Ray McCarthy, a plunger, took him into personal contract guaranteeing him $125,000 a year for two years, then insured his good health for $100,000. All these, figures that caused eyes of those in the '30s to bug out.

He had missed the first Masters, to his chagrin, committed to a foreign exhibition tour that conflicted. He arrived at Augusta in 1935 the favored professional invitee, but those of the Bobby Jones faith had concluded that the great man had merely been searching for his old tournament self the year before and now was prepared to take his proper place as a champion once more. They made Jones the favorite again at odds emitting from the Calcutta parlors and generally quoted at 5 to 1.

Sarazen played four practice rounds 17 strokes beneath par. IN-credible! He played the Thursday round of the tournament in 68 strokes, but at the end of three days found himself three strokes behind not Jones, but Craig Wood, who had unrighteously, it seemed, been bumped from the championship the year before when Horton Smith sank a long putt on the 17th green. At the end of 14 holes on Sunday, playing four holes behind Wood, Sarazen was still three strokes behind. Wood, noted for the immensity with which he delivered his wood shots from the tee, and regarded as a most handsome and amiable person, had played the last eight holes four under par.

Then Sarazen stepped to the tee on the 15th hole, which was 485 yards (before revisions lengthened it) and . . . but, no, that is for Sarazen's telling of it. Let us now move ahead, up the arduous fairway hill of the 18th hole, and into the clubhouse, there to join Craig Wood, who is accepting premature congratulations on his 282, six strokes under par, two strokes below the score Horton Smith had won with the first year, and surely, undoubtedly, by all means, a winning score this time. After all, Sarazen was out there with just four holes to play and three strokes down. He was desperately in need of more birdies in such a short distance than rationality was willing to allow.

Stories of the climate inside the clubhouse are varied and many. (Memory has an amenable personality. It bends with time, readjusts to flaws, joins in with the lie that runs through the human mind with such recurring frequency that eventually it becomes unassailable "truth.") Wood's wife had joined him. Toasts were being proposed. The winner's check had already been made out in Wood's name. Joyous was the atmosphere among the club members, excessively patronizing of the assumed winner, for Wood was a warm fellow of widespread popularity. These are parcels of some of the recountings that have emerged from the scene.

Another of the great variations is found in the number of persons gathered around the 15th green who actually witnessed the improbable shot. It ranges from a handful to 1,000. Whatever the size of the gallery, what those people saw was the sight of this golf ball descending from the ozone and then, as if directed by the hand of some celestial force disgruntled with the course of affairs, striking the earth and being gently guided into the cup. Double eagle! A five-par hole being played in 2.

In one swing, Sarazen had wiped out Wood's lead. He finished the round in 282 strokes himself. There was a play-off the next day, dismal and soggy, the one and only of 36 holes in the history of the Masters, and Sarazen won it with ease, 144 to 149. The tournament had already ended the afternoon past. Sarazen had won it on the 15th hole. Wood had lost it standing in the clubhouse.

No Masters accounting would appear representative of those times without Gene Sarazen's name engraved therein. It completed his full house of major championships. It was also the last one he took unto himself. Not that he was a fading oldster at 33. Indeed, only a disconsolate first round of 78 kept him from beating Horton Smith the next year. He tied with Lawson Little and lost a play-off to him in the U.S. Open of 1940 to reaffirm his battle-worthiness.

. . . A Man and an Island

"The only thing wrong with this place," Gene Sarazen says, "is that there's no cemetery on it. I want my bones to be buried here."

Ah, here is a man in love with a place,

a little island appended to southwest Florida only by bridge. It has a special appeal in its seclusion, for here the road ends.

Years before, when he was beginning his retreat from the wars of golf, Sarazen had been known as the "Squire of Germantown." Germantown, New York, was where he got his mail, a little squib of a community not far from Hyde Park where the Franklin Delano Roosevelts came from. Squire Sarazen was no country gentleman with clean fingernails; he was a working farmer surrounded by 375 acres of MacIntosh and Red Delicious orchards and cattle. Then one day a Manhattan type drove up in a Rolls-Royce and before he drove away, he owned the place.

The Squire had been looking, anyway, and had these 16 acres in New London, New Hampshire, in mind, about 100 miles northwest of Boston, on the shores of Lake Sunapee, not far from Colby School for Girls. No state income tax . . . adjacent to 18 holes of golf . . . and most of it lawn that he now mows himself.

But this 16-acre plot is only a place to stay when he isn't at Marco Island which he discovered 40 years ago, when the only natives were fisher people and the only public house on the island was old Marco Inn, which still sits, tropically austere in its white weatherboard exterior, at the north end where the Marco River enters the Gulf of Mexico. While the North shivered and mushed through the frigid months, the Sarazens grew new roots on Marco. Now he is the resident bellwether of golf there and lives in the constant affection of his islander-neighbors, increased to some 4,000 with the arrival of modern conveniences.

"Mary and I began coming here on account of the shelling. She collects seashells. You ought to see her collection. We walked the beaches for hours a day and came to love Marco as our home.

When I was still playing tournaments, I walked the beach three or four miles a day to get my legs in condition. Every year it was always with the Masters in mind. I wanted to be in shape for it because, now, it's the only tournament I really enjoy. Or it was until I quit playing it three years ago.

"I think Cliff Roberts was right. It was time to get the older fellows out of the tournament. I don't think we ought to be playing and shooting 80s there. They'd rather just see us around the course, I think, not on it. They want to see the Nicklauses, the Palmers, the Weiskopfs, and the young fellows play. But I'll tell you one thing, it wasn't because the old-timers were slowing up play. George Fazio and I teed off first one day and played the round in an hour and 57 minutes. The next twosome was six holes behind us. They never sent me out first anymore."

Sarazen was always one of the more brisk players among tournament professionals, and to this day, at age 74, he still moves about a golf course like an old fire-horse answering a call. When he was 71, he astonished the world with a hole in one on the 8th hole at Troon in the British Open, then followed it up the next day with a birdie on the same hole — two rounds with a total of 3 on the same hole that Arnold Palmer had a total of 11. He made the cut — that is, qualified for the final two rounds — at the Masters at the age of 67, a record of its kind. The next day he was paired with Palmer, the rains came, and his race had been run.

"The Masters was what kept me in tournament condition all those years. I'd go through my training routine every winter down here, and the last year I played I was in better shape than I was 20 years before simply because of it. Up until that time, I'd only missed two of the tournaments. I had to miss the first one because I'd signed a contract with Joe

Kirkwood for a tour of exhibitions around South America with him. I missed the 1946 tournament because Bob Hannegan, who was the Postmaster General, invited me to be his guest on a golf junket in Texas with some political friends of his, and Bob was a pretty big man in this country to be saying 'no' to, so I went.

"Kirkwood and I flew around South America in a two-engine plane. We'd play an exhibition, collect $250, and fly on to the next one. I'd heard of this tournament at Augusta before we left, but I was already committed to Joe. When I did get there the next year, I wasn't too impressed with the course. Of course, I never was a great admirer of Dr. Alister Mackenzie's architecture. I'd seen several of his courses in Europe. He had more freakish greens on a golf course than anybody I've ever seen. Even Colonel Jones, Bob's father, used to complain about it. There have been a lot of modifications in the course since then, and Augusta National isn't the same at all."

Somewhere I had read that Sarazen flares up when the subject of the double eagle is introduced, saying on one occasion, at least, "I won golf tournaments all over the world, the U.S. Open and the British Open, and you'd think that this is the only damned shot I ever hit in my life." Not so now. Perhaps with age the resentment is gone. Or perhaps there was never any resentment related to the shot, but to the way the question was asked, or to the manner of the asking.

"It was in the late afternoon, and I was playing with Walter Hagen. We had only one galleryite, and that was Joe Williams, the New York columnist. We were all talking together, not about golf, but reminiscing about old times, the tricks we used to pull on one another, and Hagen about his women. He was in a hurry to get in. He had a very special date that night.

"Just about the time we stepped on the

SARAZEN BRIDGE
ERECTED TO COMMEMORATE THE TWENTIETH ANNIVERSARY OF
THE FAMOUS "DOUBLE EAGLE" SCORED BY GENE SARAZEN
ON THIS HOLE, APRIL 7, 1935, WHICH GAINED HIM A TIE
FOR FIRST PLACE WITH CRAIG WOOD AND IN THE PLAY-OFF
WON THE SECOND MASTERS TOURNAMENT.
DEDICATED APRIL 6, 1955

Gene Sarazen, who devised the sand wedge, uses
one to point out some object of interest to Cliff
Roberts.

15th tee we heard this tremendous noise coming from the direction of the 18th green. We didn't know for sure, but we had a pretty good idea what had happened. Craig Wood had holed out for a birdie 3 which gave him a 282, and a pretty sure thing he'd win. Joe said, 'Well, I've seen enough of you bums. I'm going up to see the winner,' and he strolled off.

"Hagen and I both hit pretty good drives, and as we walked along, I said, 'Imagine that, 282. I'd have to get three 3s to tie him.' Hagen says, 'Go on and play, will ya. I want to get through here.'

"I had a caddy named Stovepipe because of the tall black silk hat he always wore when he caddied. We looked at the lie, and it wasn't too good. I said that I wanted to get the ball up so I could clear the water in front of the green. Stovepipe suggested the three-wood. I told him I couldn't get the ball up with a three-wood, so I'd take the four-wood. It was a new club which was called a 'Dodo.' I decided to toe it in a little bit for extra distance.

"From the minute I hit the ball there was a feeling in my system that it was going to be close. The ball went straight for the hole, about 235 yards away. It didn't carry the green. It carried short and rolled about 15 feet to the cup and in. There wasn't that steep incline in front of the green that's there now. If I hit the same shot today, it would roll back in the water. The only way I could tell if it dropped or not, those 20 people around the green all jumped up and yelled like hell, and one of them was Bob Jones. He had walked back down from the clubhouse to see Hagen and me finish.

"I was tied, but I still had three holes to play. I had to make 3-4-4, and I tell you they were three of the hardest pars I've ever had to make. The big test came on the last hole. I'd been playing the 18th with a driver and a six-iron every day, but a wind had come up, and I had to play it with a driver and a four-wood. I hit the four-wood past the hole — it was on the bottom — 40 feet to the upper side of the green. That green was just like a skating rink. There's no way you could hold that ball short coming back. Well, it stopped three feet short. I never even looked at the second putt, I was so nervous. It went right in the hole, and I had tied Craig Wood.

"The play-off the next day was what you'd call an anticlimax, I guess you'd say. The weather was rotten. It had been unusually cold for Georgia in the spring all through the tournament, but on Monday we had rain to add to our discomfort. Not more than a few hundred people were in the gallery, but even in the best of weather, the prospect of walking 36 holes of golf with a twosome isn't altogether inviting. Craig Wood played very poorly. His putting was off. I took the lead on the 10th hole and never lost it. I had 27 straight pars at one stretch, and I beat him five strokes, 144 to 149. One thing I was particularly proud of that week, I went the entire 180 holes, counting practice rounds and all, without anything higher than a 5 on my card.

"And what do you think we got for the play-off? Fifty bucks apiece. I had to give Stovepipe more than that. First prize was $750. The purse was $5,000. Grantland Rice presented the check. He was a member, you know. The money that's in golf today makes me think back to my father, who came to this country on a boat trying to find prosperity, and his saying to me when I first started out as a pro, 'And this golf, they pay you money to play it?' He just couldn't get the idea of being paid money to play a game."

Long since the money itself has gone out of playing the game for him, but not the gaming pleasure in it. Almost daily Sarazen is a regular on the Marco Island Country Club course, still wearing the knickers that have been as much a part of him as the white cap of Hogan. He keeps a closet full of them. It isn't easy to find knickers these days. DeFini's makes them up for him. His games are with neighbors and guests, and his ball still goes straight down the middle, just not as far as it used to go.

"That shot has made people remember me more than any tournament I ever won, U.S. Open, British Open, any of them. I was invited on the Rudy Vallee Show to describe it, and it wasn't the regular sort of thing for athletes to get attention like that in the days of radio. One of the happiest experiences of my life was doing the Shell Wonderful World of Golf on television, a series of match play events on the greatest golf courses around the world. More people saw me in one hour of it than saw me play golf in 45 years.

"When I was in the Orient doing one of them, I was introduced as the fellow who made the double eagle in the Masters. Not all the gallery was that familiar with golf, and they began to call me Chief Double Eagle. They thought I was an Indian chief."

Sarazen was closer to Bobby Jones than the other professionals. They were contemporaries. The same age. Married girls named Mary the same month of the same year. Winners in the same era. Sarazen was a frequent guest in the Jones' cottage, just off the 10th fairway.

"He always wanted me to drop in and tell him about my round. We'd have a drink or two and talk about the tournament. One day I didn't make my visit. When I came by the next day, he said, 'You didn't have a good round yesterday. You didn't come by.' Finally, visiting became too painful for him and for me. His physical discomfort increased. He couldn't come out on the course any more. It grieved me to see him in such a state, and I visited him less. When I was touring with the Wonderful World of Golf, I wrote him from all the places I visited. Mary Jones told me once, 'Don't stop writing him. He's gotten to the point he looks forward to your letters. They mean so much to him because he's seeing these places with you.'

"It was a shame to see such a gentleman as Bobby Jones go as he did, like a life with a curtain being pulled down over it."

Gene Sarazen is one of the fixtures at the Masters each spring. On Wednesday afternoon he plays the Par-Three tournament, where the Old Masters are still put on display for the galleries that'll never see Ralph Guldahl or Herman Keiser or Gene Sarazen play anyplace else. After that, he can usually be found on one of the benches on the veranda of the Lower Clubhouse, watching another Masters flow by, meeting and being met, greeting and being greeted. Always the smile. Always the knickers. He's as much a part of it, this institution of sport, as the cornerstone.

What made the Masters the Masters? The question was raised before Clifford Roberts one day. "Bob Jones, of course. His presence," he said. "Then the double eagle."

Byron Nelson putts on the 18th green, closing out the play-off for the Masters championship of 1942 as Ben Hogan watches glumly in defeat. A few years earlier they had met in a play-off for the caddy championship of a club in Fort Worth, Texas. This, Nelson also won.

Byron Nelson...New Gun from the West

Byron Nelson takes it easy on the grass with one of his most trusted friends — his driver.

"From the very beginning it was bound to be great."
— Byron Nelson

"Without reaching for a crystal ball, it is difficult to see Guldahl blowing up with any calamitous effect in round four."

O. B. Keeler gazed down augustly upon the Masters of 1937 from his perch in the Forest Hills Hotel, which sat regally above the rest of Augusta. Association with the triumphal procession of Bobby Jones had elevated him from daily drudgery as a railway clerk to international stature among the published authorities on golf.

His opinion on the approaching climax to the tournament was delivered with logic, and the wires clattered with it that Saturday night. Ralph Guldahl had picked up seven strokes on Byron Nelson that day. He had well-developed tour callouses. He knew that feel for winning, for he had won the Western Open and the prize for the professional on the American tour with the lowest scoring average the previous year. Nelson had exploded onto the scene with a round of 66 on Thursday, but he was a young and tender fellow who apparently had caught some lightning in a bottle. The realization of what he had done seemed to catch hold of him, and he went into eclipse. Now it did indeed appear obvious that Guldahl, the successful campaigner from Dallas, had the draw on the new gun from Fort Worth, no more than a week in the hire of some fancy new address up East. Imagine that Texas twang of Nelson's mixing and mingling with the dialect of Dutch country Pennsylvania when he became the pro at Reading Country Club!

What happened at Amen Corner that Sunday afternoon is now part of any recital on the Masters. How Guldahl played the 12th and the 13th holes three over par by ditching two shots, and how Nelson came right along behind him playing them three under. He picked up six strokes on Guldahl on the two holes. He won by two strokes.

"Stunning upset!" cried the Monday headlines. "Thirty-to-1 Shot Wins!" "First Surprise Winner," they all agreed. Time would by degrees remove the "surprise" element, and Guldahl would eventually get his Masters (1939), but not before finishing second still one more time to Henry Picard.

Men wore trousers with legs as big as sacks in that day, those who didn't wear knickers. "Brilliant youngster" Nelson stood shyly by at the presentation ceremonies, trouser legs flapping in the breeze, as they extolled him for his achievement, wife at his side, embarrassment in his face, then long and lean and with a prominent jaw. Keeler's logic had been done in by another former railway clerk, for that is precisely what Nelson also had been.

Oftimes history brings men together in awkward and unknowing circumstances. Just 10 years before, Nelson, as a 15-year-old boy, had followed Walter Hagen around the Cedar Crest Country Club course in Dallas, and for one shot had lent him his baseball cap, as the flamboyant one won the PGA championship. Now here was the kid, a broad-brimmed felt hat where the baseball cap used to be, taking first prize in the Masters and Hagen somewhere behind him, out of the money.

1942 was a war year. America's mind was on war bonds, at 3½ percent interest, victory gardens, and blood plasma. Ben Hogan blew in fresh from a side of 32 at Asheville, where he had won, and was, as the paper said, "perhaps the favorite,"

though Nelson had won the U.S. Open and the PGA since his 1937 Masters victory, and Hogan was still desperately stalking his first victory in a major tournament.

The war, though, overrode all thoughts, the disaster of Pearl Harbor just four months behind. Bobby Jones dedicated a driving range at Fort Gordon. Several of the pros put on an exhibition for the soldiers. Everybody was "doing his part," and newspapers were carrying on about the efforts on the home front.

Sam Byrd took an early lead on the day a headline read that Babe Ruth was recovering from pneumonia. Byrd had been Ruth's backup man as a New York Yankee outfielder before divorcing baseball for golf. Nelson shot 68-67 while Hogan was shooting 73-70, and Byrd faded to a 75 on Saturday and a 74 on Sunday. Then Hogan shot 67-70 while Nelson shot 72-73, and so on Monday at 2:30 p.m., attended by 4,000, they teed off to settle it, two former caddies from the same club in Fort Worth.

"One of the greatest shows in the nine-year history" would have to tide the gallery over for four years more. It would be that long before the Masters was back again. Nelson shot 69, Hogan 70.

The last picture Americans had of the Masters before going off to save the world for democracy one more time was that of Alfred Severin Bourne signing Nelson's winning check across Nelson's back after the ceremony on the putting green. Nelson was looking over his own shoulder smiling, but the smile said nothing. There was a certain joy overridden by a certain sadness about it all. The only one who could be certain of anything was Nelson. He would not be going off to fight war. Hemophilia. For nearly all others in the scene the future was one big flailing stab in the darkness of uncertainty.

. . . On Fairway Ranch

Highway 114 spans that vast plain from west to east. It skirts Grapevine Lake, passes by the new electronic marvel of an airport that serves Dallas and Fort Worth, and eventually loses itself somewhere in the maw of "Big D." The first noticeable bump on the complexion of Texas along the route rises along the corporate line of the village of Roanoke. Its abruptness is accentuated by the sameness of the land you've been driving and by a cluster of trees that sits on the crest of the rise. A low, rambling ranch house snuggles under the protective cover of the trees, and a stone marker on the very border of Roanoke (population 817) announces the presence of "Byron Nelson's Fairway Ranch." Pastureland seems to run for miles in all directions. Tall grass, obviously of some culture, does a graceful shimmy in the light wind. A pastoral lane invites you in, and your car comes to a halt on a gravel turnaround, surrounded by the trees, which are Spanish oak and hackberry. The comfortable feel of the landed gentry's life is all about you.

"I guess the best thing that ever happened to me was hard times," Nelson says, dug down deep in his relaxing place in the den, terazzo floored and cooled by an air-conditioner that hums somewhere out of sight. "I was working as a file clerk at the Fort Worth and Denver City Railroad — that's the Frisco Line now — and when times got hard in the '30s they started laying people off. I didn't have but two years seniority so I was among the first to go. Otherwise, I might still be working for the railroad."

Byron Nelson is no rancher by name and association with the Texas image alone. He is a practicing rancher, with about 150 head of cattle and a first-name relationship with the county agent. The county agent had just been there that morning, accompanying the editor of a magazine leaning toward the agricultural life, and they had focused on the Rancher Nelson as a developer of an admirable strain of grasses, not the Golfer Nelson.

For years, to the public, he has been a dry, wind-swept voice analyzing professional golf shots over the ABC Television Network at tournaments from some of the world's most sophisticated addresses, but always he has homed in on Fairway Ranch when his "dress-up" work was done. Here he and his wife, Louise, a Texarkana girl he met in Sunday school, have made their nest since the late '40s.

The afternoon is peaceful and stiflingly hot, discouraging vigorous endeavor. Except for the occasional crisp chimes of a wall clock every quarter-hour, there are no distractions. It is a mellow moment for tripping about among the glories of great moments past.

"When they say I was the first 'surprise' winner in 1937, I suppose I was. Sort of like a 'rabbit' today. I know I was surprised, too. I'm still the second youngest player that ever won the Masters, and I was the youngest until Jack Nicklaus won his first. I was playing with Wiffy Cox the last round, when I overtook Guldahl. Wiffy was pro at Congressional Country Club in Washington then. Well, I always thought that was where it started, there on the 10th hole. I was playing right behind Guldahl, and he birdied the 10th hole. Now, if I don't birdie it, I'm four down and eight holes to go.

"I got my birdie right behind him, and I remember Wiffy Cox saying to me, 'Kid, I think that's the one we needed.'

"Over the years I've come to think of the 12th and 13th as two of my favorite holes, and not because of the 2-3 I had there that day. I've never put many shots in the water on the 12th, and this time I went straight for the pin and only had about an eight-foot putt. I had a good drive on No. 13, and it was no wild gamble going for the green. When I eagled it, I'd picked up six shots on Guldahl on two holes, but I always think of the 10th hole as the pivotal one."

Above the mantlepiece is a framed needlepoint reproduction of his four winning rounds in the Masters of 1937, done from the authentic card of the time ("Caddy fee 75¢" in the upper corner). To the right of the fireplace is a replica of the plaque that was dedicated in 1958 at "Byron Nelson Bridge," crossing Rae's Creek at the 13th tee. The rest of the room, wall and shelf, is a ledger of Byron Nelson's awards and triumphs and honors in golf.

"They didn't have the green jacket ceremony in those days. I don't know when it started. Bobby Jones handled the presentation, and I was standing there feeling nine feet tall just to think that Bobby Jones was making an award to me.

"What got me my invitation was a match play tournament in San Francisco just after Lawson Little had won the U.S. Amateur and the British Amateur two years in a row. I was the least known of the qualifiers. It was played on the course at the Presidio (an army post) where Lawson's father was a colonel, and when I beat him decisively, it got headlines all over the country.

"The year of the play-off with Hogan, I was very fortunate to get a tie. My foot slipped on the 18th tee Sunday, and I pushed my drive into the woods on the right side of the hill. I had no opening to the green. The only way I could get there was to take a five-iron and hook it up toward the 10th tee. I almost knocked it in for a 3, but I made my 4 and got into the play-off.

"I woke up the morning of the play-off with an upset stomach. I was just overexcited, and when I got that way I couldn't keep anything on my stomach. Ben was staying just down the hall from us at the Bon Air, and he stopped outside the door on the way to breakfast. When Louise told him I was sick, Ben said, 'Oh, oh, I don't want to play him today.'

"Well, I was so upset, I hit a pine tree and went into a bunker and took a 6 on the first hole. I lost another stroke on the 4th hole when my tee shot hit the trap. Then I began to feel better. The excitement was gone. I was scared now. The next 11 holes I was five under par. We didn't say much during the round. It was a pretty big deal for both of us, so we kept our minds on our work and our mouths shut."

He is 63 now. His career as a competitive player has been over more than 25 years. He was spectacular while it lasted. No other man has ever won 11 tournaments in a row on the professional tour. Nor 19 in one year. Nor will it ever be done again, as it was in 1945. Nor would his stomach ever have been a stomach again if he had not ceased. Sometimes no matter what he fed it, it was rejected. Once his nest was feathered, and he could see the comfortable life assured, he quit the pressure of his game in 1946 one step ahead of ulcers.

Yet, on the outside, he had always seemed so calm. So in place. The wild, the undisciplined, the player given to the distilled juice of the grain, in him such a condition could be accounted for. But it is remembered that as Nelson stood before his interviewers after the Masters of 1937, he had said, "I actually haven't ever touched a drop in my life. I don't drink and I don't smoke." As far as I know, this is still true.

"Another funny thing happened between Ben and me one year. They always had this Calcutta before the Masters at the Bon Air. That's an auction where people 'buy' players in the tournament, and, naturally, the best players go at the higher prices. I walked into the back of the room just about the time Ben's name came up.

Now, this was before he was very well known. He hadn't become, I guess you'd say, a big star yet. Nobody was bidding on him, so I bought him for $100.

"Next day at Augusta National, Ben looked me up. 'I hear you bought me in the Calcutta for $100,' he said. I told him I did.

"'I've been playing great lately,' he said. 'I wonder if you'd sell me half of it.' So I sold him half. Well, Ben played just awful, 78-80, or something like that. Our investment went down the drain.

"I played the Masters 27 straight years. Finished in the top ten 15 out of the first 18. There'd been a tradition when Jones was playing that he was paired with the defending champion on the first round and the leader on the Sunday round. When Bob quit playing, they did me a real honor. He and Cliff Roberts had taken a liking to me, so they asked me to take Jones' place. It humbled me. I don't know why they picked me, but I always thought it was one of the greatest honors I've ever had. It came to an end the year Ken Venturi almost won as an amateur and took the lead into the last round. He was sort of my protégé, and they decided that it wouldn't be fair for him to be paired with me — not that I'd help him during the round, but he ought to be paired with somebody else. I've always felt that if we had been paired, Ken would have won because it would have been a calming influence with me along.

"My relationship with Jones was not any closer than most of the others my age. He was older, and the greatest name in golf to my mind, and I looked up to him. I never had any really close ties with him, but something comes back to me now about him at the Masters Club Dinner one year. There had been a lot of complaining about pin placements, especially on the 6th hole, where it can be impossible if they put it in the upper left-hand corner. Anyway, there was a lot of jabber about it, and Bob listened until he'd had all he wanted, I guess. Anyway, he opened up:

"'You fellows make me sick,' he said. 'Do you realize that you should be rewarded with a birdie only on an exceptional shot? You're not content if you're not shooting for a birdie all the time. Did it ever occur to you that you're not supposed to birdie 18 holes?' I don't think I have to tell you, a great hush fell over the room. We all held him in awe, you see.

"The story of the Masters to me is, of course, Jones. And Gene Sarazen's double eagle. No doubt in my mind but what that had a lot to do with getting it on the public's mind. And the kind of course it is. No roughs. No tricking it up. Not a lot of bunkers. A course for shot-making and club judgment and putting. You play the ball to the right position, and on those water holes you better pick the right club. That's where the Masters is won and lost. And it puts a premium on putting. From the very beginning it was bound to be great."

The follow-through of the fluid swing of Craig Wood, champion of both the Masters and U.S. Open and one of the strongest players off the tee of his era.

Byron Nelson (L) and Craig Wood look over Ben Hogan's shoulder at a card game in an upstairs room in the Manor Clubhouse. Obviously, it's a moment of relaxation for everybody but the grim Hogan.

Awaiting his turn, Jim Ferrier rests on haunches on the lower edge of the 18th green as Byron Nelson putts. The year was 1950 and the big Australian was on his way to losing his lead, and the tournament, bogeying five of the last six holes.

Peter Oosterhuis, the Britisher with the Dutch name, blasts out of a bunker on No. 13, the Azalea hole, backed up by a bank of same.

The green of the magnificent 10th hole, as seen through the yoke of a tree.

Above: Green on green — Hubert Green putting on the 10th green, Dave Stockton watching.

Left: Beauty suspended — hanging basket of petunias on Manor Clubhouse veranda.

Sam Snead...Mountain Boy

Sam Snead chipping up to treacherous 14th green in 1970.

"They can't close the Masters book yet on Slammin' Samuel Jackson Snead, who rose up out of Ashwood, Virginia."

He came out of the backside of the Appalachians, a Depression kid from an area which was already depressed before the Depression reached it. Where man lived by his hands, tilling a reluctant soil or burrowing into the earth for the black gold that fills his lungs with infectious silt. He was a budding legend looking for a place to burst into blossom.

"Sam," they called him. Plain Sam. Until the fluid perfection of his swing and the vast span of earth his drives covered demanded something catchy. Superhumanizing. Glamorizing. He became "Slammin' Sam." The name has been as durable as flint rock, as the personality it represents. Nearly 40 years later both man and nickname are still current and going.

Samuel Jackson Snead emerged from Bath County, Virginia, as some rustic who might have been created in some fanciful narrative. Ashwood isn't on the map. It has no traffic light. Only a smattering collection of weatherboard houses, most of them in need of paint, and a store or two. It's somewhere around Healing Springs, Millboro Springs, and Hot Springs, which is the resort where the elegant gather. Mitchelltown was the high school. Here Sam was some kind of Li'l Abner. A Bunyan of the hills. He was the whole athletic program. Center on the basketball team. Halfback on the football team. All nine positions on the baseball team. Anything he entered, he won. Summers he played on a semipro team with old men against the tough mining company teams. Ran the 100 in 10 flat, which came in handy when

95

mining town toughs accepted defeat ungraciously. And all the unofficial mountain recreations, such as coon hunting and squirrel shooting. If you needed a fox, he'd catch it, bare hand.

Of the "society" sports, tennis reached him before golf, except as an economic measure. As a sprig, he caddied at Homestead Hotel where all the swells stayed. It not only brought in coin, it spared him the milking and plowing and mucking chores. He played tennis with such accomplishment that when a tournament came to the fancy resort hotel, he played in it and almost beat the Czechoslovakian professional, Karl Kozeluh. As for golf, when he played it, his equipment was hacked out of hickory, a limb with a big elbow knot on the end for a club head. He laid out his own green in the farmyard with tin cans for cups. When the game came his way seriously, he was just as much a natural with store-bought equipment. Soon he was on the road representing Greenbrier Hotel, Homestead's rival across the state line in West Virginia. He leaped upon the nation as a hillbilly sensation. A strong, salty-tongued, drolly witty, supple fellow, athletically attractive and crowd pleasing. He grabbed hold of the tournament tour by the throat his first time around and never let go. As his head turned to unadorned skin, his trademark became the coconut straw hat.

When he won the Oakland Open early in 1937, he caught the attention of Augusta National, and an invitation to the Masters found him as he headed East. The story circulated that Greenbrier had given its professional the week off to play the Masters, but without pay. Coming to $10. After Snead had won at Oakland, he was shown his picture in the *New York Times* accepting the champion's check. "Well, I'll be damned. I wonder how they got my picture there. I never been to New York in my life," he is supposed to have

said, in a voice that seemed to come out of a mouth filled with syrup.

All the crafty promotional hand of a man named Fred Corcoran, then the director of the professional tour. Snead laughs at the memory of such Corcoran didos today, for it is Corcoran who said, "Sam has made a million playing golf and saved two million," and it is Corcoran who helped him make it later as his personal manager.

Snead finished 18th at Augusta, but ahead of two-time champion Horton Smith. Ahead of Lawson Little, Jr. Ahead of Paul Runyan. Ahead of Gene Sarazen. Also ahead of Robert Tyre Jones, Jr.

Thus began the most enduring competitive association of man and Masters, running from 1937 to _____ (fill in the blank). No other has played 36 Masters. No other has played 31 COMPLETE Masters. In 1975, a bad back took him out after nine holes of the second round. No other has played 133½ rounds of the Masters. And still counting. Only Byron Nelson has played as many as 100; Arnold Palmer has played 81; Jack Nicklaus 61; Gene Sarazen 97.

The year of '39 became known as the year of Guldahl against Snead. While Sam sat in the clubhouse with a 280 on the board, a new record, Guldahl played the incoming nine holes in 33 strokes, three less than par, caught and beat him by a stroke.

By the time Snead finally won one in 1949, his 10th attempt, he might have reached the conclusion he wasn't supposed to win it, were it not for his Presbyterian attitude. There is some question as to whether this attitude applies to the U.S. Open. Snead's unrelenting pursuit of the Open and the tragedy of his failures are as much a part of the American legend as the purple mountain majesty and "Remember the Maine." It is the only big one that got away.

In the Masters of '49, he completely

dissolved all suspense. He played the last two rounds 10 under par, 67-67. He won by three strokes. The next five years were Hogan, Snead, Hogan, Snead, with one interruption in 1950 by Jimmy Demaret, who insisted on becoming the first winner of three and broke the rhythm.

It might be charged that Snead picked up the scent of money the year of the first $20,000 purse in 1952. Actually, the story of that Masters was as much of Hogan's collapse as Snead's perseverance. They went into the Sunday round in a tie for the lead. Hogan learned it was possible for him to three-putt — three times — and shoot a self-destructive 79. Even the ogre 12th where he found water — and almost sixed — couldn't kill Snead, who shot even par and finished four strokes ahead of Jack Burke, Jr., who moved up with a 69.

Now to the grand climax, or the ultimate in Olympian fate. Almost as if by some deific ordinance, the two crusty old warriors are found locked in a post-mortem combat for the prize in 1954, a year otherwise remembered for (1) foul weather and (2) an amateur, Billy Joe Patton. William Joe went tearing out into the lead on Thursday as if he didn't have any better sense than to expect to win it on Sunday. And would have if he, this mountaineer from North Carolina, had not taken wild, low-percentage gambles on holes 13 and 15 and wound up on the wet side, and outside, both times.

Meantime, Hogan and Snead finished 75 and 72 and 289, unartistically one over par, and ran the show into a fifth day. They were fiercely competitive on a personal basis. Rugged rivals of the time. As different as salt and sugar. Never one to spend social time with the other. And it bears repeating, thrown together here as if by some sinister judge who decreed that there should be a final settling of affairs.

The play-off round went to Snead, 70 to 71, and from the 16th hole on in, it was a stroll. So he became the second three-time winner. Neither ever won again. They came close, Hogan in 1955, Snead in 1957. But neither won again.

Hogan had an era that bears his own name, roughly from '48 through '55. Snead never had one. He has won more tournaments than any professional who ever lived, but they have been spread from the '30s to the '70s. He spread-eagled others' eras. Sometimes he was hot. Sometimes he was cold. Forty years is no one man's era; it's a bunch of eras. He's 64 years old now, but he's always back answering his tee time at Augusta. In 1974, he was 72-72-71-71 at age 62. They can't close the Masters book yet on Slammin' Samuel Jackson Snead, who rose up out of Ashwood, Virginia.

. . . One of the Swells, Now

This is another kind of world, awash in the startling sunshine and the glaring reflection of the sand along the east coast of Florida. Palm trees and banyan trees and a sea grape hedge hold against the encroachment of wind and sea. The crags and the gnarly pines and the trails awinding, the mountains of Virginia are lost somewhere in the long ago, though only yesterday Sam Snead and his wife, Audrey, and their son, Jack, had driven in from their other home in Hot Springs.

It's an annual migration, and it has been so for 11 years. Eight months in the mountains, the other four by the sea at Highland Beach, one of those little clots of high rises and temporary refuges so numerous in South Florida, this one pinched in between Delray Beach and Boca Raton. Sea-front property is too precious for many single residences. Sam Snead's is one of a few. It sits 21 feet above the ocean, shielded from public view, rendered almost unnoticeable by the beehive towers of condominiums that distract passersby. It has a kind of style and affluence that a little fella who whittled his first golf clubs out of hickory limbs and slept two boys to a bed never knew was out there. He'd seen the high society folk at the Homestead Hotel in Hot Springs, their fancy cars and their frills, but he was part of them only as an attendant, a bag strapped across his scrawny back, responding to the command of the possessor of a spastic swing who some day would pay $100 an hour for Snead's favor.

"I was six years old the first time I caddied. The driver came up to the top of my head. A little colored boy came by one day and said, 'C'mon, go with me, boy, you and me, we make lots of money.' It was two and a half miles to the golf course, and I walked it every day, then walked around the golf course toting that bag," Sam Snead says. Sunlight burns through the picture window to the sea. A maid vacuums the rugs in the background. Jack is setting up his telescope by the window to bring in the seascape.

"I played every kind of game in high school, but I took to golf because you didn't have to depend on anybody else. First time I ever went to a tournament, they took the high school golf team to Woodberry Forest for the state meet. I'd never seen sand 'greens' before. I hit 'em with a shot, and the ball would bounce a mile high. I finished third, but I won the driving contest — with a three-wood."

His repute as a player spread, and after he'd won the West Virginia Open and the West Virginia PGA, one round of 61 astonishing the mountain country, he set out upon the tour, "Me and Johnny Bulla in a '36 V-8 Ford." So he put behind him the scrimping days of teenhood, when he jumped center against Orville Welch, six-foot-six ("I always outjumped him. His feet left the floor but his head never seemed to get any higher."), and ol' Ben Long ("He was all bones and knobs and it

hurt to block him."), and horseshoes with his uncle, and golf on the "goat course" with the same uncle who never counted whiffs.

"The Masters wasn't very much thought of in those days. I was playing at Greensboro, and I'm with Fred Corcoran now, and I get this invitation and I'm not going down there. Well, Fred gets me a practice round with Bobby Jones on Monday, and it's getting late Sunday and looks like we're not going to be able to get there. So he charters this plane, a little old single-engine job, to fly us to Augusta. That pilot used a road map to find his way. Corcoran kept trying to cross his legs, and he was so nervous he couldn't get them crossed. I went to sleep. I think I shot a 68 playing with Bob. I also played a couple of exhibitions with him, one in New Jersey and one in Florida. Bob was a good driver and a good fairway wood player and a good chipper and putter, but, you know, he was weak on long irons. If you'll look back over his record, you'll see that those par threes gave him fits.

"I stayed at the Bon Air the first year, and I had the misfortune to get a room next to an amateur player and his wife, and they fought every night. Jimmy Demaret's running up and down the hall. He couldn't sleep. There for years he didn't get any sleep at all. He was a walking drug store. He had a one-hour pill and a two-hour pill and a blockbuster that really put him out. He always gave the appearance of being calm, but he was all nerves. Hagen never slept any either."

Nearly 40 years later Snead has come to Florida to get his game in shape to get back to the tournaments. It's not that pressing part of his life and livelihood anymore, but he still plays 10 to 15 tournaments a year. Staying active keeps his name active. Wilson Company says his name is the biggest money-maker it has ever had. One line of clubs bearing his

Sam Snead putting, illustrating his latter-day sidesaddle style.

endorsement brought him $152,000 in 1974. Barbells and a weight-reducing machine in a closet — indicators that condition isn't automatic with him. Old man of the mountain refusing to concede an ounce to time.

"There wasn't anything I could do in '39 but sit there in the clubhouse and wait for Guldahl to come in. He'd beat me out of the Open the year Bobby Cruickshank thought he'd had it won at Oakland Hills. Cruickshank's in the clubhouse celebrating, 'At last, I won a major tournament.' Then I come in and catch him, and while we're both sitting there having a drink, Guldahl comes in and takes me by two strokes. So here I am sitting in the clubhouse at Augusta and Guldahl's catching me again, and beats me by a stroke. I caught a few people in my time, too.

"I don't remember too much about the first year I won. They had the green jacket the first time. Johnny Palmer was leading after the third round. He was playing right behind Jim Turnesa and me, and I see him knock this one two feet from the hole for a 3 on No. 11. Then I finish 2-4-4-4-3-4-3. I think that was the toughest that course ever played. They'd just changed the grass on the greens.

"The year Hogan and I went out tied on Sunday, '52, I think . . . well, I always thought that 12th hole wreaked more havoc on the leaders than any hole on the course. I told J. C. one time, 'Don't pay any attention to that air over your left shoulder. That wind comes down Rae's Creek, around those pines, and comes back over your shoulder. Always play it long on No. 12, or you'll go in the water and it'll cost you.' "

Uncle Sam was an oracle. A few years later, leading the Masters by a stroke, nephew J. C. Snead switched from a six-to a seven-iron on No. 12, his tee shot splashed in Rae's Creek, and he lost the Masters by a stroke to Tommy Aaron.

"They say the short holes have won it for me, and I guess they're right. But that year I won it and put it in the water at No. 12. When I dropped, the ball rolled into silt there and was half buried. Then I come up short on the bank just across the creek. The ball had a gob of mud on it. I'm lying three, and it looks like I'm going to take a 6. I chipped and that thing started wobbling toward the hole with that mud on it, wobble-dy, wobble-dy, wobble-dy, and it went in the hole.

"I told O'Brien, my caddy, 'Well, we ain't lost it yet.' (You know, that sucker had 18 children!)"

As memories, though, Snead's Masters recollections are harbored in his mind either in a distinctly vivid state or obscured behind a veil that closes out all but the peak details. They are checked out disconnectedly, rarely ever in sequence, but as associated with some particular man or circumstance. All, that is, but for one — the play-off round with Hogan in 1954.

"I could go back and put the pins in the greens and put our balls on every green for you. And how many putts we had. This fellow at the PGA tournament last year comes up to me and says he wrote this book about the Masters, and he tells me this story about the round. He says, 'Hogan never missed a green and you missed five.' I told him, 'You don't know what the hell you talking about.' "

There is a silence. Then as if an invitation has been issued by that silence, he begins a recounting of this dramatic confrontation of golf between the two finest players of that age over 21 years ago.

"The 1st hole, we're both on the green in two and two-putt. The 2nd green, I'm on in two and Ben's in the bunker, but we both get down in two. Now we both hit the next hole in two and down in two putts again. I three-putted the 4th hole, the par three, and I drop back one. We both hit No. 5 in par figures. No. 6, I make a two, about a six-footer, and we go back even. We both two-putt the next hole. Now No. 8, I'm just above the hole and have an eight-footer for a 4, and we birdie it. We both hit the 9th in two and two-putt, and we make the turn even.

"We move over to No. 10 now, and he's on the green. I chip in for a birdie. He's got a putt, one of those three- or three and a half-footers with a little quick break, and he takes five minutes to putt that thing, but he gets it in. We both hit No. 11 and get our pars. Now the 12th, I hit the green right at the flag, and he sees where my ball hits. My ball bounces up and buries in that second trap. They had two traps back of the green. He don't even shoot at the flag; he shoots at the center of the green, right over that little trap, so he'll be in that valley. He knows I can't get down in two. He don't know I'm buried, but he knows he's not going to take more than 3. I got it on the green out of that bunker and two-putted. He chips up and makes his putt, and he's one up.

"Now we play the par five and I'm over that little rise with my drive, and he's to the right of me. He comes over and looks at my lie, and it's not too good; now he knows I'm going at the green, but he sees the lie I've got. Now he can, if he hits really a stomper, get on the green, put it on the left side. Well, he thinks I'm going to go at it and hit in the water, so he lays up. I knock it on with a two-iron. He don't even get it on the green with his chip. He almost puts it in the water. He's on the fringe. I hit my putt, and it looks like it's about to go in for a 3, and here's my caddy, O'Brien, standing over it hollering, 'Git in, git in,' waving his hand over it. I almost lose my breath for I'm sure he's going to knock the ball in the hole with his hand.

"I say to O'Brien, 'O'Brien, if you had a-hit that ball with your hand, I was going to bury you right on that green.'

"So we leave No. 13 and I'm one up. Now the 14th, I'm right behind the hole. I got about a 13-, 14-footer. The pin's way up in that left corner. He doesn't hit a good approach, or something. There's a little mound up there and it comes off, and he's just on the green, way down in that right-hand corner. He's got about 80 feet. He got up and down, though, and we both get 4s. On the 15th, I hit a three-iron to the green, and he hits a wood and goes over the green about 20 feet. Now, the first time I ever see him do this, he uses a putter — he's on the verge of getting the yippies — and he damn near puts it in the hole. I almost three-putted, but I got my bird.

"Now on the 16th hole, we're both down in the bottom to the left, and the pin's up in that right-hand corner. My putt leaves me out about six or eight inches, and just as I start to knock it in a guy hollers — must have been about 10,000 people there — 'Miss it!' Everybody turns around and looks at him, and I know if he could find a hole he'd crawl in it. But I don't miss. Ben don't hit a very good putt and leaves himself about three and a half feet. I say to O'Brien, 'Maybe he can miss one for us. I missed one for him.' Dogged if he don't give it a quick snatch and miss it to the right. Now I've got him by two.

"On No. 17, I'm on top of the hill with my drive and he's not quite on it. But my ball has rolled onto a divot. You know, one that had dried up. It's lying there like a rocker. If I touch it, well, the ball's going to jump. I say, 'What am I going to do? This thing is liable to go 50 yards, or it might go a hundred.' So I say to myself, 'It's not there. It's just not there.' I take a swing on it just like it's a normal shot, and it flies on the green pretty as you please and I'm dead center. Hogan's second shot is a helluva shot, but it goes over the green, but we both get pars.

"Now we go to No. 18. They'd

A fairway shot by Sam Snead in 1975, just before an ailing back forced him to withdraw after 27 holes.

watered it up there where the drive hits. My ball is lying where it's muddy, but not enough where you can drop it. He puts his second shot down on the lower level of the green, and the pin's up on the top. Now a son-of-a-gun gets it down in one putt from there has got to be better than Houdini. I take a four-iron, and then I say to myself, 'If that thing flies out of here to the left, I can take any number.' So I switch to my three-iron, because if it goes in that trap to the right, it's okay, for I'm a good trap player, but no way it's going to the left. I can't take more than 5. So I hit one low in there, a screamer, into that trap. Now everybody's saying, 'Now, now, now . . . .' But Hogan's way down here, see. He made a good putt to get 4. But I zip it out about five feet from the hole. Well, there's no sense trying to be a hero now. I just dog that thing up to the hole and tap it in. I didn't try to hole it, and I win by one stroke."

The yard man comes. Snead wants to talk to him about the chinch bugs in the St. Augustine grass, pocked with sickly looking patches of brown. The compressor on the air-conditioner has rusted out. One of the awnings has developed a sag. The property on which the house sits slopes back from the beach, and the first floor is mainly a den, with a beach entrance on one side, a bar as the dominating facility, a pool table to one side, and Jack's traps and drums set up in a corner.

The route out leads through the den and back to a general catch-all room, trophies in a case, a wilderness of fishing tackle stacked in a corner, ancient Scottish golf clubs in an elephant-foot bag, which he draws out and displays. Centered on the wall, though, in the most prominent position, is an item in which its owner takes exceeding pride. It's a mounted fish.

"That's a 15-pound bonefish. I caught it on a 12-pound line. Ain't it a beaut? That sucker was a record for several years," he says.

British Open champion, PGA champion, Masters champion three times. The trophies catch the eye again on the way out. These attest to a man who has captivated this earth mass with his deftness at golf, a classic artisan. Yet, here captivated himself by the fascination and the uncertainty that comes with dropping a line in mysterious waters.

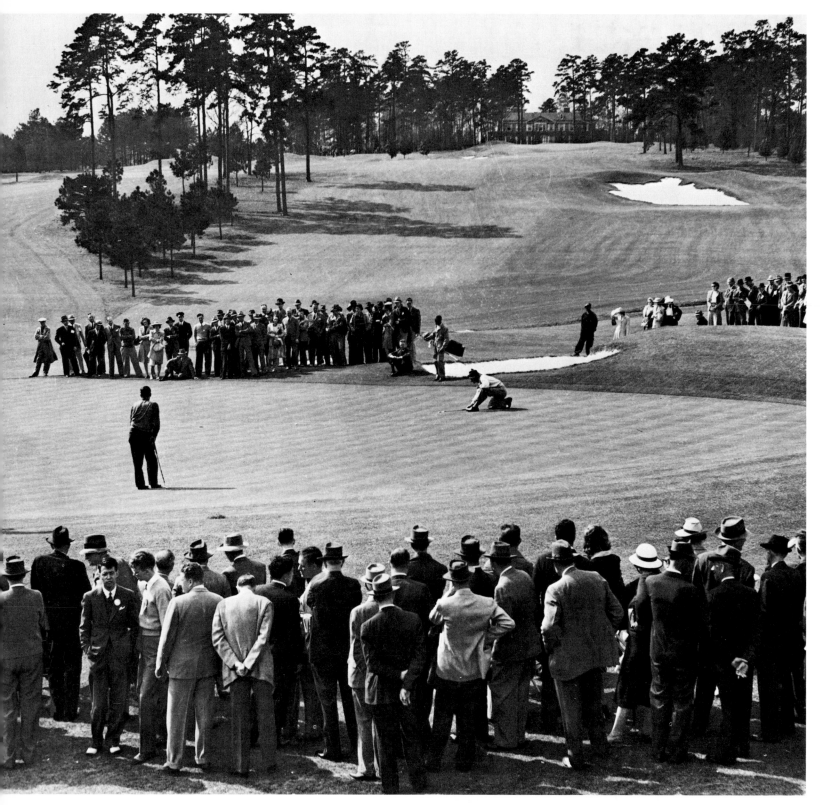

Jimmy Demaret lines up putt on 9th green during the first round in 1941, paired with Bobby Jones, who leans on his putter.

A Jimmy Demaret chip shot to the 8th green before the mounds were removed from the long, uphill hole.

Bobby Jones, Fred Corcoran, onetime PGA tour director, and Jimmy Demaret (L to R) having a chat.
Note the rakish chapeau, one of hundreds from Demaret's collection.

"I got my ideas about colorful
clothes from watching my father
mixing his paints in the garage."
— Jimmy Demaret

It is appropriate that James Newton
Demaret should have won the Masters
twice on Easter Sunday, for he was known
as the peacock of the fairways. A one-
man Easter parade of color. Flamboyance
of dress became such a trademark of his
that the glare almost blinded the world to
the fact that he was one of the most
masterful golfers of the time.

Galleries kept track of his sartorial brilliance almost as closely as they did his
scores. He startled them in conservative
old England when he showed up for a
Ryder Cup match one year wearing a
chartreuse sweater, strawberry colored
trousers, and a screaming green cap. He
owned at one time at least 300 changes of
costume. When he packed for travel, it
was as if a haberdashery were changing
towns. He came out of Texas looking like,
and being what the rest of America
expected of, a Texan. The only variation
from the old stereotype was that he was
poor for a while, but not for long.

He launched his career of tournament
golf by catching an MKT Line freight
from Galveston to Dallas to play in the
Texas PGA championship in 1934. His
luggage for that trip was spare — an extra
shirt and a toothbrush. He won the tournament — and he won it five more times,
as a matter of fact — but the money
wasn't enough to pay his hotel bill, so he
made his exit by a fire escape.

Demaret had his chance to make a
clean break from the depression-stricken
world of golf about this time. Among his
other splendors was his voice. He had a
rather nice, wholesome, big band Irish-
Spanish-Dutch tenor. The "Old

Maestro," Ben Bernie, was singularly impressed as he made one of his night-club tours through Galveston, when Galveston was a wild and wide open town, and offered him a job. But golf won. Demaret breathes a sigh of relief these days when he tells of turning it down. "Just think," he'll say, "I might have to be living like Dean Martin."

He set out to make his fortune, and while it wasn't instantaneous, it was inevitable. After he'd won the Los Angeles Open in 1939, he was approached by the PGA tour director, then Fred Corcoran, with the stimulating news that he was being invited to play in the Masters. He'd heard of it, but he wasn't too sure what it was. He knew of it as Bobby Jones' tournament. He didn't have anything else to do that week, so he decided he ought to play in it. He made no big splash in the Masters of 1939. It turned out that he and Jones tied for 33rd place.

When he came back the next year, he was armed with a confidence he'd never known. He had won five tournaments on the winter tour before he reached Augusta. With $6,000 earned in prize money, he felt rich for the first time in his life. He had turned the front nine Thursday in 37 strokes when he read on the scoreboard that Lloyd Mangrum had done it in 32 playing ahead of him and was bringing the back nine to its knees. That's when Demaret turned it on.

He played the next nine holes in 30 strokes, which was a record then and is still the record now. It has been tied but never broken. Mangrum completed a round of 64 that day, a record for the course, but the next two days Demaret chipped away at the other Texan's lead until he went out for the last round ahead by a stroke. He was never really pushed on Sunday, and with 17 pars and one birdie, he stretched his lead to a comfor-

table four strokes, converting the last few holes into a jaunty stroll through the afternoon. His 72-hole score was 280, his margin over Mangrum four strokes, which was a record to that time, and his prize was $1,500, more money than he had ever seen in one bunch in his life.

When he won again in 1947, and again in 1950, golf became convinced that the caddy shack had turned out another jewel of a player. That was Demaret's origin in golf, just as Hogan and Nelson, too, had emerged from the ranks of Texas caddies. Until he learned that there was money to be made toting golf bags, little Jimmy had assumed that he would follow his father in the painting, carpentry, and general household handyman work. There were nine Demaret children, and Jimmy and a brother had to pitch in to help as newspaper vendors on the streets of Houston. Jimmy was walking by an army base golf course one day and stopped to watch soldiers knock the little balls around. He'd never seen that funny game before. Pretty soon he was back, and when he learned that he could make as much money caddying for a day as he could peddling newspapers for a week, he switched.

Once he was promoted to the pro shop, he began moving around Houston, from club to club, until he came to River Oaks, the swankiest place in town in those times, and met the man who he says "made me a golfer." One recognizes the name of Jack Burke, Sr., mainly because of Jack Burke, Jr., who hit his peak when he won both the Masters and the PGA championship in 1956. When Sr. didn't have Demaret tied to duty, Jr. was demanding his attention as the baby-sitter, and in time would come to figure prominently in his life.

At Augusta, Demaret was not a threat again until after World War II had ended, and the world had settled back into place. The year was 1947, and by this time the fellow who liked to call himself "Houston's Ambassador to the World" had burst into full bloom in raiment, and even the flowering shrubs of Augusta National were hard put to match him.

He was equally as impressive with golf clubs in his hands. He shot a 69 the first round and was never out of the lead from start to finish. That was also the year he led the PGA Tournament Tour in money won and the year he put his name on the Vardon trophy for the lowest scoring average for the year.

In 1950, it was a different story. Demaret finished his round on Sunday with a total of 283 strokes, but Jim Ferrier was on the course needing only a journeyman's 38 on the back nine to win. Demaret was pretty much resigned to second place. Never one to closet himself in the clubhouse and mull his plight, Demaret headed for the broadcast tower adjacent to the 18th green and listened to and talked of and watched the tall, stooped Australian play home to his doom. Instead of a 38, Ferrier soared to a 41, and Demaret had to come down off the radio tower to step into a green jacket. It was historic. He had become, purely by default, the Masters' first three-time champion, and to illustrate his good faith and appreciation, he finished his share of the presentation ceremony by singing the lyrics of a song called, "Do You Know How Lucky You Are?"

This bundle of happiness and joy wasn't finished yet. He tampered with a little more history in 1962. Off the tour and playing only on occasion, Demaret returned to the Masters at the age of 51 years, 10 months, posted rounds of 73-73-71-70, and became the oldest player to finish as high as fifth.

Though Demaret was the first three-time champion of the Masters, he came up short of the international recognition, the awe and the admiration of technique that fell to his contemporaries Hogan, Nelson, and Snead. He accumulated none of the other royal titles to support that stature he'd gained on the course at Augusta. He sat in the clubhouse at Riviera in Los Angeles in 1948 with a new U.S. Open record for 72 holes by his name, but before the afternoon was out, Hogan had replaced his 278 with a 276, and that was as close as Demaret ever came to that championship.

Demaret never pursued professional glory, never courted such ambitions with the unrelenting ardor that marked Hogan's style. There was some life to be lived, some good times to be had. It was not uncommon that he should turn night into day. He greeted many a dawn personally.

On the outside, he was hearty, happy-go-lucky, loose, and supremely at ease, it seemed. It was a front. He was churning on the inside. He was a bunch of jangled nerves. He was a light sleeper. Five hours was his average night's rest. He could barely remain immobile any longer.

On occasion, Hogan, who was his close friend and confidant, chastised him for his habits.

"Do you realize how many more tournaments you might have won if you'd trained yourself, kept better hours, and not done all that partying?" Hogan asked his friend Demaret once.

"Do you realize how many I might not have won if I hadn't gone out and relieved those tensions, Ben?" Demaret said to his friend Hogan.

. . . In Living Color

Champions Golf Club is about a 20-mile drive west of Houston International Airport through flat Texas lowlands of no particular distinction. Not an oil derrick or a cow to give the scene a Lone Star prop. Shopping centers and residential subdivisions crop up in clusters along

State Route 1960, like nodes on an artery, and construction is still booming.

When the U.S. Open was played there in 1969, the road to Champions was blacktop, two lanes wide. The club and its community had their own little corner on isolation and seemed immune to encroachment.

Now the road has grown to four lanes and habitation thickens as you approach the main entrance. Champions springs up like a surprise on the right as you come upon one of the holes of the Jackrabbit course. The other course, on which Orville Moody won the Open, is called Cypress because Cypress Creek winds in and out among its holes.

Residential streets at Champions are named for famous golf courses, and as you pass Bermuda Dunes Drive, the clubhouse spreads out before you, red brick and roomier than it appears from the outside. The men's locker room is as big as a gymnasium, and not infrequently here can be found the two Champions, namesakes of the club, Jimmy Demaret and his partner, Jack Burke, Jr. Since the time Demaret worked for Jack's father, the two have been close, though in the earlier baby-sitting years it was a relationship of caretaker and charge. Demaret is 10 years the elder.

The two Masters champions got together and formed their own club in 1957, and the name was a natural evolution. Burke played on competitively for several years more while Demaret turned to television commentary and traveled the world with Gene Sarazen as one of the voices of Shell's Wonderful World of Golf. Now they share an office at the club, desks in opposite corners, and it has been a compatible arrangement with no traces of ruffled feathers.

The peacock of the fairways is costumed rather mildly on this winter day, brown knit sport shirt with white trim along the collar, brown trousers with diamond-shaped checks of a gentle nature, and a very calm pair of executive shoes. Perhaps it seems mild only because golfing gentry took his cue and caught up with him in flashy course dress several years back.

"When I first started playing, a golfer's attire was an old blue serge suit so worn it was shiny, an old white shirt that was not fit to wear on the street, and old shoes with spikes screwed in the soles. That was before we had deodorants, and you could smell a golfer 200 yards away.

"I guess I got my ideas about colorful clothes from watching my father mixing his paints in the garage. You couldn't go to the store and buy any color you wanted then; you had to mix your own. I used to stand and watch him, and some of those colors stuck with me, I think. Anyway, I began to wonder why you couldn't liven up golf with some color.

"It wasn't easy. I began going to 554 Fifth Avenue in New York, where all the movie stars, Clark Gable, Adolph Menjou, and the best-dressed actors got their clothes. I told them I wanted some slacks made out of that purple and pink and yellow cloth, and they said, 'Those are ladies' colors. They'll laugh you off the course.'

"I told them I'd laugh along with them, just make me up some slacks. Then I'd take a piece of the cloth and send it to Brockton, Mass., and have Footjoy make shoes to match. I got my hats from San Francisco, from this fellow who ordered them from France and Switzerland. That's how I became a flashy golfer, and it all started in my father's garage."

Demaret made his plunge into competition unattended by flamboyance.

"How'd you like to start out to your first tournament in a boxcar? Ben Bernie, the band leader, gave me the money to make the trip to Dallas to play in the Texas PGA in 1934. He was playing at a place called the Balinese Room in Galveston, owned by Sam Maceo, and they both took an interest in me. I was afraid I'd need the money for other things, so I hopped a freight and as it turned out, it was a good thing that I did.

"In those days it cost $25 to belong to the PGA, collected on the 1st tee. I won the tournament, and it was a good field. Ben Hogan, Byron Nelson, the Mangrum brothers, Dick Metz, and Ralph Guldahl all played in it. I set a new record for the tournament, and when they gave me the check for first place it was $25. I'd broken even. I had to catch another freight to get back to Galveston. I read the other day that Johnny Miller had become the ninth millionaire golfer on the tour. Can you imagine how much a Hogan, or a Nelson, or a Mangrum would make if they were playing in these times?"

A priest sticks his head in the door to wish him a good day. Champions is the only golf club in the U.S. with the blessing of the Pope. A scroll on one of the walls bears testimony to this, and priests play free on Mondays.

"Now to get to the Masters. I was playing well on the tour in 1939, but I didn't play well in the Masters. The next year I was getting ready to tee off on No. 10 when I heard that Lloyd Mangrum had a 32 on the front nine. I hit a one-iron about six inches from the cup on the 10th hole and birdied it. I birdied the 11th hole. That was a dogleg to the right in those days, a great little hole. I almost knocked it in the hole on the 12th but birdied it. I birdied the 13th with a long putt.

"Now I came to the 15th hole. It wasn't quite as long as it is now, but it was the same type hole. I hit my second shot across the lake, but the ball trickled back into the water. By this time I knew that Mangrum was in with his 64, so I took off my right shoe and rolled my trouser leg up to the knee and took a whack at it, just hoping to salvage a 5 instead of a 6. The ball landed on the green, about 50 feet from the pin. I holed the putt, and Ed Dudley, whom I was paired with — he was the pro at Augusta — came over to shake my hand. I finished the backside with a 30 and won the tournament, and those two shots at the 15th hole were the keys to the whole thing.

"After you've won three Masters, it isn't easy to look back and try to remember how sweet the first one was. As far as I'm concerned, the second and the third were just as big a thrill to me. One of the bonuses of winning in 1940 was that I was privileged to play the first round with Bob Jones the next year. It was the tradition then, the defending champion always played with Bob Jones the first round. I was scared to death when I saw the pairing in the newspaper. Neither one of us fared very well. He shot about a 79 and I shot a 77.

"Something special I liked about the Masters in those days, and all the tournaments, was that the gallery walked on the fairways with the players. They spoke to you and asked if you remembered some aunt or cousin from Oshkosh, and it was just a neighborly kind of atmosphere. They had gallery marshals to control the crowd. The people didn't run around like cattle. But then along came ropes and they pushed the crowds back and golf became like baseball and football, where spectators were kept at a distance. It just took something away from the game for me.

"One of the finest compliments any two golfers ever were paid came when Byron Nelson and Ben Hogan played off for the Masters in 1942. Just about the whole tournament field stayed over to watch them, and one of the reasons was, we could walk along and kibitz shots and talk to each other, and to Ben and Byron as they played. I remember seeing Tommy Armour, Ralph Guldahl, Jimmy Thomson, Willie Goggin, Bobby

Cruickshank, Jug McSpaden, and Henry Picard, just to name a few, in the gallery that followed Byron and Ben.

"Why did we stay? Well, they were about the two greatest players in the world at the time. It was like a match race between Secretariat and Ruffian, you might say. It drew a huge gallery. I noticed the other day that the Masters is going to the sudden death play-off. I like that.

"Oh, I remember funny little things from these early days. I remember Ralph Guldahl stopping to comb his hair before every putt in 1939. It was just a nervous habit of his, something to relieve the tension. I was playing with Hogan when he three-putted the 18th green and lost to Herman Keiser in 1946. The greens were slick as ice in those times, before they introduced the new grass. I remember Skip Alexander used to say, 'This is the only tournament where we start off putting on grass and wind up putting on sand.' Another year they had a hail storm, and we had to stop play while they swept the hail stones off the greens.

"We had some pretty high old times around Augusta back then. There were still some places with gambling in the back room and good food and a lot of good friends. We used to go to a place called the Colonial Club, out by the Forest Hills Hotel, and we were out there Saturday night during the 1947 Masters when I noticed it was getting pretty late.

"'I've got to get some sleep,' I said. I'd had a few belts, and when I got back to my room at the Bon Air, I forgot to lock my door. I was sound asleep when the door burst open and Jug McSpaden and Toney Penna charged in and said, 'Get up, we've got to have another drink!' Then threw a bucket of ice water on me.

"I was leading Nelson by three strokes, and when I got to the course the next day, I wasn't sure I was going to be able to play. I sat down under a tree. It was where Ike's Cottage is now. They had bowling on the green there then. I sat under that tree until they called me to the 1st tee. I hit my first shot in some brush on the right. I sliced my second shot, but I managed to get it on the edge of the green, and I got my par. I thought I was going to shoot a thousand, but I got around with a 71 and beat Nelson by two.

"I never was much for a lot of sleep, anyway. I was afraid I'd miss something good. I know I was criticized by people who said I didn't know whether I wanted to be a nightclub entertainer or a golfer. I knew what I wanted to be. I never was serious about being a singer. I liked people and I liked to be where the life was. I knew all the band leaders in those days, and I sang with Ben Bernie, George Olsen, Bernie Cummins, even Lawrence Welk, of all people — but just for fun, never for money."

His singing brought him note to note with some of the most notable larynxes of the time. He sang once with Bing Crosby on the Kraft Music Hall when that was one of the top radio shows in the network ratings. When he played tournaments in Cleveland, he always managed to work in a few numbers with Sammy Watkins and his orchestra at the Hollenden Hotel, standing in for a big-nosed Italian kid, the regular vocalist, who stood growling and fidgeting in the wing.

"Now every time I see Dean Martin he tells me how I tried to beat him out of his job with Sammy Watkins."

It was fun. It was la joie de vivre. It was the Demaret flair. The people in the Valley down in Texas — that's down where the Rio Grande approaches the Gulf of Mexico — can still catch his act on their lucky nights, when Demaret happens to be relaxing at his place, called Los Compadres. He and his cadre of friends, often including Bing Crosby, Phil Harris,

Don Cherry, or Rusty Draper, pitch in on the podium at the Valley Inn and let the good times roll.

Demaret had a second chance to change his course back in an age when tenors were in demand, and the price was out of sight for the times. It was then and there that he pledged his troth with golf, for only a man in love with the game would have turned down such a gold-plated proposition.

"The William Morris Agency offered me $1,500 a week to play two shows a day at the Paramount Theater in New York. I'd played golf with Lou Clayton at the Hillcrest Country Club over in New Jersey — that's Clayton of Clayton, Durante, and Jackson — and Lou had paved the way for me.

"That wasn't only a lot of money for those times, but I hadn't been on the tour too long — it was before I won my first Masters — and that was more than you got to keep if you won a tournament a week. It would have been a tremendous thing, but I turned it down, which shows you how much I wanted to play golf."

When he captured a third Masters in 1950, it was an artistic triumph whose value and impact have been unrighteously watered down by passing time and subsequent events. Byron Nelson and Horton Smith had become playing guests by that time. Sam Snead had won only one. Ben Hogan had yet to win. And nowhere in sight was there any hint of the forthcoming of an Arnold Palmer or a Jack Nicklaus. It was the Masters Demaret recalls most vividly for the par-five holes and, in particular, No. 13 on the round of Saturday.

"I was playing with Roberto de Vicenzo from Argentina, and I hit my tee shot out to the right. I was staring a 77 in the face, and that would have knocked me completely out of it. Jim Ferrier already had a lead of five strokes on me. I had a downhill lie, not too good, but I

took my two-wood and cut my second shot just across the little stream in front of the green, and the ball ran up toward the hole. I got a tremendous hand from the gallery around the green, and when I got closer I could see why. My ball was about two inches from the hole.

"I got my eagle there, to go two over par. Then I birdied the 15th and the 17th. Instead of a 77, I had salvaged a 72, and that turned that whole tournament around for me. Made no difference what Ferrier had done on Sunday, when he bogeyed five out of the last six holes, if I hadn't had that recovery on Saturday, I wouldn't have been close.

"The amazing thing about that tournament was that I played the par-five holes 10 strokes under par, and I don't think that has ever been done. I played the 13th 4-3-3-4, two eagles, six under par. I was one over par for the rest of the tournament."

By contrast, Ferrier needed 19 strokes to play the same hole. Demaret won the tournament 283 to 285, but won it on the sideline in the helpless state of any other spectator.

"I went up in the radio tower and sat with Harry Wismer, who was doing the broadcast, after I finished. I had realized as I played the 18th hole that I had a chance to win if I got down in par. I ran my first putt downhill about eight feet past the hole. I was playing with Norman von Nida, a little Australian, and I said, 'Norman, I'm going to putt it out.'

"I putted it right quick and it went dead center into the cup.

"I was sitting in the radio tower while Ferrier was playing the last four holes. I don't know who was suffering worse, Jim or me. I was lipping with Wismer, trying to be light-hearted about it.

"'Nice to see old Jim make those bogeys,' I said. 'Good going, Jim.' I wasn't pulling against him. I was pulling for me.

"Before you go, I want to tell you

about one of the greatest shots I ever made in golf. I made it on the 10th hole at Augusta in 1947, and it barely got a clap from the gallery. Golf fans like to see shots hooked around trees or out of rough or over hedge rows. Those shots look great, but they're easy for a pro.

"My second shot came to rest on some pine straw just off the edge of the 10th green. There was a little bed of needles under the ball, and I had to be careful where I stepped, or it might move, and I couldn't sole my club. I took a seven-iron, hit that ball just perfect with a little spin on it, and it rolled up to the hole so I could get my par. The gallery never even gave me a hand. Those people just didn't know how fast my heart was beating."

Jimmy Demaret is gradually becoming a pioneer in the history of the Masters, one who brought a fresh spirit to the tournament and to a game that was needing such a venturesome one to get it out of its mortician's wardrobe. He returns these days, but mainly for the Masters Dinner, which he was never privileged to host because it was not created until after his three winnings. After the dinner and a couple of days of practice rounds, he flies back to Texas and watches the rest on television.

"I was kidding Cliff Roberts one year at the Masters Dinner; I said, 'Cliff, you've built a bridge for Nelson and a bridge for Hogan, and you've put up a plaque for Sarazen. I won the Masters three times; don't you think you might put my name on one of these little green outhouses?'

"Everybody has theories about what made the Masters, and I have mine. Of course, we all begin with Bob Jones. That's unanimous. But, in my opinion, what also made it was the combination of geography and timing — baseball and spring training. Being located where it was, the Masters got the attention of all the big-name sportswriters on the way back home from spring training in Florida: Grantland Rice, Joe Williams, George Trevor, Henry McLemore, Red Smith, Arch Ward — they all stopped over to cover the Masters. They put the Masters on a pedestal. They built it up. That's how the Masters made its big name in my book. It stands for what golf ought to stand for, and the press got the point across."

Two Texas neighbors on the 10th tee, Byron Nelson driving and Ben Hogan watching. The graduates of the Glen Garden caddy ranks had come a long way.

114

Right: Jimmy Demaret accommodates for a gag shot by whispering into Lloyd Mangrum's ear in the day when ties were still worn on the course.

With deep intensity and firmly set jaw, Ben Hogan strikes a tee shot on No. 15.

Jack Burke, Jr., 1956 winner, awaits his turn on tee.

Ben Hogan and wife, Valerie, awash in smiles after Augusta victory.

Ed (Porky) Oliver emerges from bunker bordering 18th green after historic 1953 round with Ben Hogan. Their best-ball score was 31-29—60.

Ben Hogan...a Last Hurrah

Ben Hogan exercises his orderly style teeing off on the 2nd hole.

" 'Hawk,' swooping, hovering over a tournament field as if every player is his prey."

The white pancake cap under the fierce glare of the sun gives off an ethereal glow as it first appears, rising above the sharp slope that forms the fairway approach to the 18th green. It symbolizes its wearer, the small, almost insignificant figure that appears now, head, shoulders, waist, and then the knees that often fill him with pain and cause him to walk haltingly.

The cap never waggles from side to side but moves only in a straight line toward his ball. He strikes it again, then resumes his walk that tells of fatigue and ache, now approaching relief. Underneath the bill of the cap there appears a slight trace of a smile, for in that vast crowd forming a people amphitheater around the green, something rather strange, most uncommon, is astir. Everyone is getting to a standing position, and a rising current of applause is topping out into a roar like the sound of a waterfall into a chasm.

It is as if they sense they are witness to the last great flash of some millennial comet making its farewell streak across the sky. Ben Hogan, 55, is finishing one of the rounds of golf that America will take home and put under its pillow. "Bantam Ben," in American jargon. "Wee Ice Mon," they called him worshipfully in Scotland. "Hawk," swooping, hovering over a tournament field as if every player is his prey.

He has been out of it since he won the Colonial Invitational in 1959 on his home course in Ft. Worth. He won his last Masters 14 years previous. The show is over. But before they dim the lights and the orchestra puts away its horns, one more flourish for old time's sake.

Hogan was playing out the final strokes of a round of 66 — 30 of them on the last nine holes. No one has ever played those nine in less. But more than anything else, the galleries played them with him. "So knowledgeable of golf," as they say of Masters spectators. So knowledgeable here that they helped with the sound effects. On every green from the 10th through the 18th it was the same. Standing ovation after standing ovation. As if they were seeing one last gallop by Man o' War. Red Grange scoring four against Michigan one more time. Johnny Weissmuller wringing one more gold medal out of the pool. No more emotional round of golf has ever been played, and if there was a dry eye left in Augusta, it was unseeing, its heart unfeeling. No one asked, but should they, his playing partner was Harold Henning, a quite appropriately unobtrusive South African.

It seemed for the longest time that some wretched witch of fate had it worked out that Hogan would never win the Masters. By the time he did, Byron Nelson had beaten him to it 14 years earlier. And had won it again in 1942 in a circumstance that wrenched Hogan's pride. They had tied after the regulation 72 holes, and Nelson beat him by a stroke in the play-off. They were the same age. Had grown up as caddy rivals around Ft. Worth. Jimmy Demaret had won it three times! They were best friends.

Twice Hogan had been second. (Four times overall.) Once, Nelson had beaten him in a play-off after Hogan had made up eight shots in the last two rounds. If that wasn't enough, try 1946. The sallow, sad-faced Herman Keiser, the "Missouri Mortician," sat in the clubhouse and won while Hogan surrounded the hole on the 18th with three putts. Not the Ben Hogan you know, you say!

Finally, in 1951 it came after that calamitous collision with a bus along one of those long ribbons of concrete that make up Texas highways. Skee Riegel, a reformed amateur, led after two rounds and, after three, was joined by Sam Snead, Hogan one stroke back at each juncture. On Sunday, Hogan blew them out with a 68, figuring it was Snead he would have to beat. Instead, it was the reformed amateur who stayed close. Snead shot an 80.

The next year, Hogan led again after the first two rounds, then was gone. Vanished. Out of sight. Like a blip on a radar scope. But in 1953 he was back. Ben Hogan was back like Ben Hogan. He came as close as any man has ever come to shooting four rounds of Masters golf at Augusta National in less than 70 strokes each (70-69-66-69). He won by five strokes. He broke the 72-hole record by five strokes. It was four days of golf fit for a museum, something for a man to remember.

One of the pungent memories of that year, one that commutes between the comic and the heroic, is that of Ed (Porky) Oliver, waddly, florid-faced, unathletically formed, beside Hogan, compact, trim, finely tuned; Oliver throwing a 67 at Hogan on the Saturday round and Hogan throwing a 66 back in the same pairing. Oliver, one of the finest players of the time, would be dead of cancer in five years. Hogan was taking aim on his peak year.

He came closer than anyone ever had to that elusive measure of perfection established by the press, the professional Grand Slam. Later, he also won the U.S. Open and the British Open, and to this day golf's lordly, beetle-browed, black-robed judges for posterity look upon Ben Hogan's Masters of 1953 as the finest 72 holes of golf played in the first 100 years of their game.

In Fort Worth his name is still spoken with an awed reverence, as if he is some shah living in splendorous seclusion behind some great palace wall. He's Ben Hogan, executive, now. Age 63. Most of the hair is missing from his pate, except for a few wisps carefully lacquered down. The growth along the temples and the nape of the neck have developed a salt-and-pepper touch of distinction. The face is a bit fleshier, but the unmistakable look of the eagles, those investigative eyes, still dominates his being.

West Pafford is an industrial street that shoots off old Granbury Road across the railroad tracks in the southwest of town, not far from Texas Christian, not far from Colonial Country Club, where he won five tournaments. The pavement is rough. The rest of the industrial neighborhood, busy with the bottom line, pays no heed to its illustrious incumbent. Out of General Steel, across the street from AMF Ben Hogan Company, come the harsh sounds of men and metal clashing.

In the parking lot is a light tan Eldorado, "Hogan" (the product) prominently displayed on a sticker across the rear window. The building is not seemingly large, but inside it sprawls. Also, inside it is blessedly cool, for Fort Worth suffers in its August torpor. It's hot enough for Texas sirloins to broil on the hoof. Somewhere in the distance a diesel horn hoots like a surly moose.

The lobby displays the Hogan line of sporting wear — see the prominence of the old-fashioned white cap? — and golfing gear. It's about time for the new line to come out.

Ben Hogan himself comes forth, dressed in a conservative grey suit, and speaks warmly. He stops to introduce Bill Sovey, the president of AMF Hogan. Hogan's title is . . . well, he's Hogan. Then he introduces his secretary, delight-fully Irish, delightfully matronly Mrs. Kelly, who buffers him against the prying world.

"I'll tell you about Dublin," he says as we move on into his office. He speaks of the town of his nativity, about 90 miles southwest of Fort Worth. His mother moved her little brood to the city after Ben's father died. "It used to have three banks when I was a kid. Now it has one."

His is the largest office at the end of the hallway, carefully furnished with antiques and old golf prints, with several pictures of himself and President Eisenhower, and other friends of Augusta, unpretentiously intermingled along the light brown paneling. His desk is big enough to require the services of a captain, and in his swivel chair behind it, Hogan himself seems to fit the role. Then as he shifts about in the chair and gets comfortable, it seems he grows smaller, dwarfed by the high back, like the "Bantam Ben" who used to stride the fairways at Augusta National. And he talks of those exciting times.

"An invitation to the Masters was a very special thing even in those days. A part of it was Bob Jones. An invitation to the Masters was an invitation to play with him for several years. But it also had a great field and a great golf course, all those things that make a tournament great.

"I had played in the Masters before, in 1938 first, but very poorly. I was a bad player when I was a kid. When I was a young pro I still couldn't play. I guess you'd call me a late maturer. I was naturally left-handed, but the only clubs I could get were right-handed. I started out playing cross-handed. I used to sweat when I'd get that left hand up there. I finally just had to overcome it by force.

"Byron and I had met in a play-off once before, when we were caddies at Glen Gardens here in Forth Worth. We were both 15. Caddies were allowed to play one day a year, Christmas Day. The ladies of the club put on the tournament. We tied and Byron won the play-off. As I recall, they gave us both some kind of golf club for prizes.

"Now, here we were 16 years later in a play-off again, for the Masters championship, the two caddies from Glen Gardens. I recall that starting out I picked up two strokes on the 1st hole and another by the time we reached the 5th. For the next 11 holes I was one under par, but I still lost five shots. That's how well Byron was playing.

"The 10th hole sticks in my mind. The pin was cut short to the left. I played for it, but my second shot was just short of the green, not bad position, but it took me three strokes to get down. If I get down in two I win, I think. Yes, I remember that as the big thing.

"By the way, when you go to visit Byron you'll go right by my new club, just about two miles down the road from his ranch on the other side of Roanoke."

His present project borders on an obsession, just as playing the game once did with him. With Joe Lee, the eminent course architect and a man easy to be with, he is approaching the final touches on 36 new holes of golf. Hogan has graduated from Colonial, the second most exclusive club in Fort Worth, to Shady Oaks, the most exclusive, to his own, The Trophy Club. It's a good 35 miles from his office in a part of Texas with some trees and some roll to it.

The name was an ordeal. He would have nothing that even hinted of some other great course. No St. Andrews of Texas. Or Muirfield Estates. Or Carnoustie Acres. It was his wife, Valerie, who came up with "The Trophy Club" one evening. Never one to squander a word, he responded immediately, "I like it." The case was closed. And so the insignia is grooved into the entrance columns along Highway 114, along with

his likeness wearing the traditional cap, two miles from Byron Nelson's ranch.

Now we turned again in time to riffle through his memories some more.

"What happened to me on the 18th green in 1946 caused them to change its contours. I thought my approach was going to hit the flag, but the ball landed and stuck about 15 feet above the hole. The greens were so slick you could almost hear them crackle in those days, which I liked, as a matter of fact. But there was simply no way of stopping the ball from above the hole. I just touched it lightly, and it started rolling so slowly I could read the name on it. It barely missed the hole and rolled on four feet below it. The break had been left to right coming downhill. It had to be right to left coming back. It wasn't. It broke right again.

"The next morning several members went out and tried the same putt I'd had above the hole. Not one of them could make it stop. That summer they cut it down and gentled the angle.

"In those days, you leave yourself 30 or 40 feet from the hole; it was almost impossible to get down in two. The grass is better now. Not that winter rye but a new hybrid that leaves a cushion. Now you can lag a ball and stop it by the hole.

"I remember that 18th hole again in 1951, what had happened before. The pin was in the same position, but I didn't shoot for it. I aimed a six-iron just short of the green and came to rest just off the putting surface. If there was anything I didn't want, it was a downhill putt. I took my pitching wedge and just bumped it up six inches from the hole, knocked it in, and won with a stroke to spare.

"1953, well, that's as good as I can play. Of course, Saturday was the key round. Porky Oliver was an easy fellow to play with. Some are easy, some are hard. Demands on second shots at Augusta are just out of this world. If you're playing with a fellow whose game you know, the flight of his ball, you can read off it. He's using you, you're using him. That was the way it was, playing with Porky."

We are easing up now to the year of the 66, 14 years after he had won his last Masters. After one 14-year stretch of never finishing out of the leading ten, he had had to become accustomed to something less than his old perfection. Hogan is basically no sentimental person. So much has been made of that recurrent flash of brilliance, the emotional nature of it, that one might nervously wonder if it did not border on the mawkish to the man himself after so long. It becomes apparent that it did not.

"You talk about something running up and down your spine, that round of 66 . . . well, it's hard to describe the feelings a person gets under those conditions. I'd felt those things before. I'd had standing ovations before. But not nine holes in a row. It's hard to control your emotions.

"Those things reassure you.

"I think I played the best golf of my life on those last nine holes. I don't think I even came close to missing a shot."

"I suggested the Masters Club one night in 1952 while we were just sitting around shooting the bull. I thought it would be good for those who'd won the tournament, who talked the same language, to get together at dinner and talk of old times and great moments. They thought it was a great idea, especially since I was the defending champion and would pick up the check. It's still set up just like the tournament, on an invitation basis. Jones and Roberts were the only two from outside. Now only Cliff is.

"Let me tell you why it's one of the greatest golf tournaments in the world. As I said, Jones gave it initial impetus. But it's the only tournament I know where they welcome all suggestions about how

to improve anything, the course, the atmosphere, down to the fertilizer. Anything for improvement. What will it do for the tournament? Is it helpful? Is it good?

"They weigh these things carefully. They have a committee of 15 or 20 members who do this. They don't miss a thing. After the tournament they have a meeting, and they write a complete report on it, and they study corrective measures, and all summer while the course is closed, the work goes on. With that sort of system, you can't fail to have the best tournament."

As he moved along in age, Hogan made the Masters his "opening of the season," and trained for it, literally drove himself as hard as any major league baseball team preparing itself in Florida. He, too, repaired to Florida. Each winter he and Valerie would pack off to Palm Beach, not for the glittering social atmosphere — although one year they did share a holiday with the Duke and Duchess of Windsor in the residence of a mutual friend — but for the training site. Hogan was, and is, a great admirer of the Seminole Golf Club, and there he practiced and played arduously.

One of those springs, though, he practiced and he played and he trained and he slaved over his game, but it never came up to Ben Hogan standards. When it came time to leave, he and Valerie set their course for Fort Worth, not Augusta. He would not put himself on public display, of all places, in the Masters, to be gazed upon pityingly as some relic, some dear old gentleman who once used to know how to play this game.

"I haven't been able to get back the last few years. They've invited me to get involved, but I haven't had time. I will one of these days. I'll get back."

"Give my regards to Broadway," George Archer seems to be saying after sinking a putt on 13th green on his way to winning 1969 Masters.

Lee Trevino strokes an impressive approach toward 9th green, divot airborne, ball suspended above bunker. Ike's cottage is in background.

Girl-watching — another of the Masters' popular auxiliary sports.

Framed by stately forest, Jack Nicklaus delivers a fairway shot.

Arnold Palmer tracking a putt on 16th green in 1964, the year he became first four-time winner by a comfortable margin of six strokes.

Arnold Palmer...a Kind of Immortality

Arnold Palmer at rest — leaning on his driver at the 10th tee.

"There's no doubt that the Masters established me."
— Arnold Palmer

Arnold Palmer and the Masters came together at a providential point in their existences, and they grew together, one nurturing the other. It was on the fairways and the greens of Augusta National that Palmer found a kind of immortality that comes to few, one that can be lived and breathed, be seen by eyes that enjoy, be heard by ears that hear, and is not left to some epitaph delivered over a departed spirit.

He was, himself, the spirit of the Masters for a decade, the most exciting decade the tournament has ever experienced, during which he won four times and never finished worse than second, or five strokes behind the leader. This was some kind of goal too remote for a boy growing up on a company golf course ever to have included in his dreams. Sitting between the legs of his father, he rode the mower over the course of Latrobe Country Club, which his sire served as combination greenskeeper and professional. From Milfred Palmer, known as "Deke," he learned his playing manners.

He would station himself on a fairway about 120 yards from a drainage ditch that lady members particularly feared and make the girls a deal that some could not refuse.

"Knock it over the ditch for you for a nickel, m'am," he'd say. You'd be surprised how much spending money a bright-faced boy of seven or eight could earn with such chivalry in those times.

Today he owns the course. He also owns other courses. He owns a name that the public pays for on products ranging from golf balls to Cadillacs. He is a millionaire several times over who owns and flies his own jet plane. He has been on a first-name basis with presidents. He opened the door to his home in Latrobe one morning, and there stood a former president making the delivery of a birthday present. It requires no exorbitant imagination to surmise that Dwight D. Eisenhower and Arnold Palmer were pals.

He has become that kind of idol to which the public holds a deed of ownership. He falls into the same category of cynosure as DiMaggio. As Crosby. As Sinatra. As Elvis. As Namath. As Ali. Just being someplace he draws a crowd.

He was the first athlete with his own "army," unofficial and unarmed, and to this day, unsurrendering. There have been imitators — "Nicklaus' Navy," "Lee's Fleas" — but none of these lasted. "Arnie's Army" still musters today wherever he plays and marches to his tune. It was in Augusta that "Arnie's Army" began to take shape in 1958, while he was winning his first Masters, and rallied full strength in 1960 and tramped beneath the pines, baying at his heels, stirring up swirls of dust and fracturing the air of dignity that the Tournament Committee strives so righteously to maintain.

There isn't one among us who pursues golf and who has stood on the sacred acres of Augusta National who hasn't heard the woolly-voiced cry, "Go git 'em, Arnie!" split the air.

This is not to contend that the Masters has ever been average or methodical. From the times of Horton Smith to Jack Nicklaus, there has always been excitement but usually the refined Cornell-vs-Brown kind of excitement. A certain chaste exuberance. When Palmer arrived, he brought out the bleacherite gregariousness in the gallery.

His timing was expedient. He showed up when television coverage of golf tournaments was beginning to broaden, when the old shepherd's game needed a dramatic actor for its new stage. When he smashed across national television, even in black and white, charging home and winning the Masters, followed by the U.S. Open in 1960, the Palmer legend was founded. The screen was his. Every time he was on it he became a performer playing a role. It was brilliant outdoor theater. He became America's ideal. Across the greens of the country, golfers began to hitch up their trousers, tug at their gloves, squint prune-facedly at their putts, and attack with a machete-swinging drive, envisioning themselves as ol' Arnie at Augusta.

Palmer had already won in 1958. He had played the Masters since 1955 when he was allowed to exercise his invitation as the U.S. Amateur champion, though he had already turned professional. But it was in 1960 that he captured the fancy of all America.

Palmer launched himself quite impressively in 1955 when he shot 72-69 on Saturday and Sunday and finished tied for tenth place, for which he collected the sum of $690; not enough to fuel his jet for the trip now, but enough to make the drive home to Latrobe full of fun and promise in the old trailer he towed that year.

In a back room scene two years later, upstairs in the Manor Clubhouse, Bing Crosby was stoking his pipe contemplatively and fixing his mind on affairs as the sun set on the fourth round Sunday. He had been watching his first Masters and had seen Doug Ford win while half the field was still on the course.

"I still like that young Palmer's temperament," Crosby was saying. "He is going to be a fine golfer one of these days."

By that time, Palmer had already won the Canadian Open, his first tournament breakthrough, and two American tour events. But the convincer was to be the Masters. Even as he won at Augusta, though, it was never without predicament

A typical Arnold Palmer drive, full of the physical force and facial fierceness which captivated thousands of admirers and coalesced them into his personal "Army."

or controversy. The first three Masters Palmer won, he was sorely pressed, and if it wasn't one thing, it was another. There was the incident of the plugged tee shot on the 12th hole on Sunday in 1958. Heavy rains had turned the course into a sponge, and when his shot imbedded back of the 12th green, about a foot below the bunker, a confusion of rules arose, leading to some theatrics that could only be witnessed from afar by the press and gallery on the other side of the creek behind the yellow restraining ropes. Palmer and the official assigned to the hole engaged in a dialogue, like two actors on a stage, but it was only a pantomime to the spectators, morbid with curiosity. This is what was taking place:

Seeing the buried situation of his ball, Palmer called to the man wearing an armband. "I'm going to clean and drop this ball," he said.

"Oh, no," said the official. "You can't do that."

Palmer pulled a piece of paper from his pocket and pointed to the line that read: "The imbedded ball rule is in effect."

"Yes, but that's only through the green."

Palmer said, "Yes, that's right."

Assuming agreement, he started toward his ball again.

"But here at Augusta," the official said, "that means only through the fairways."

"Oh, I beg your pardon, through the green means anything except the putting surface, the teeing ground, and the hazards."

At this point, the discussion became somewhat heated, resulting in Palmer finally saying, "Well, you don't mind if I just play a provisional ball, do you?"

Even here the official was reluctant to concede but finally gave in. Palmer was seething by this time and attacking the plugged ball with a wedge, managed to move it only 18 inches into some casual water. He dropped now, chipped toward

the pin, took two putts, and got down in 5, a double bogey. He moved back now to his original position, below the bunker, dropped a provisional ball, chipped close, and made a par three. Now, he was either a stroke up on or a stroke down to Ken Venturi, with whom he was paired, depending on which ball was ruled official. The wait was agonizing. Not until Palmer was playing the 14th hole did an official arrive from headquarters, hear the particulars of the case, overrule the greens official at No. 12, and sustain the 3.

By that time, Palmer had converted his smoldering fury into an eagle at No. 13. But before he could be jacketed, he still had to stand by and watch Doug Ford and Fred Hawkins miss putts of 12 to 15 feet which would have tied either of them with the leader on the 18th green.

He arrived at the 17th hole a stroke behind in 1960, needing birdies on two holes not conducive to birdies, and produced them in a scene that turned Augusta National into an explosion of exhilaration. He was floundering when he reached the 16th hole in 1962, desperately in need of rejuvenation, not to mention two birdies again, even to tie. Once again he produced and forced his way into a three-way play-off on Monday to win his third Masters victory.

Each of the first two years, '58 and '60, the other player in the scene was the luckless Ken Venturi, still looking for the one that got away in 1956. In '62, Palmer's victims were Gary Player and Dow Finsterwald. In 1964 it was the course. That was the year he grabbed the brass ring on the first day and never let go. For once he won in a gallop with 276, at that time a score surpassed only by Hogan's 274 in 1953.

There is always the mourning for those that might have been, and in Palmer's case over those six stirring years, it might be said that his record was four won and two he should have won. The 12th hole became the demon who rose up and slapped his face in 1959 just as it had been his benefactor the year before. He drowned his ball in Rae's Creek, lost the lead when he required six strokes, and Art Wall fled by him in a flurry of birdies — five on the last six holes — and won. Palmer came charging into No. 18 leading by a stroke in the Sunday dusk of 1961, hit the bunker with his approach, took double bogey 6, and lost to Gary Player.

That was the day that he said, "I thought 6s were for other people."

But 1964 — ah, what a lovely year for his "Army." The Palmer troops had a four-day picnic on the grounds, a romp over the green and through the trees. He played the first round in 69, sharing the lead for a day with Gary Player, the South African, and Kel Nagle, the Australian who would carry Player a year later to a play-off in the U.S. Open before losing. But Palmer took the lead by four strokes on Friday with birdies on four of the last six holes. He extended it to five strokes on Saturday with another 69. He played a patient round of 70 on Sunday and completed the rout.

"Arnie's Army" was so carried away it went to the air that weekend. They poured out of the hills and the towns of the Carolinas, where Palmer had schooled and golfed at Wake Forest College, and they congested the course in numbers never before seen. The Masters steadfastly refuses to issue attendance figures, but based on the number of vehicles in the parking lots, free-lance estimates ran to 35,000 for both Saturday and Sunday.

As they surged about the course in glee Saturday afternoon, spectators had their attention directed aloft when a light plane appeared overhead towing a sign that read, "GO ARNIE GO." It was an astonishing intrusion that triggered great elation among the "infantry." Again on Sunday afternoon the plane appeared, towing this time a sign being a bit more direct: "GO ARNIE 68."

Investigation later revealed that a recent alumnus of Atlanta Federal Penitentiary, turned to flying on his release, had been the pilot. The pilot was serving three clients who paid him $100 for the Saturday flight. He was a Palmer fan himself, and, being so caught up in the thing, said, "The one on Sunday was on the house."

That was the day, also, that Palmer stood on the 18th tee with his playing partner, Dave Marr, facing that tunnel of a fairway that opens up on the gallery, shoulder to shoulder, around the 18th green, feeling safe and comfortable. Six strokes in the lead and relaxed at last. His consideration now turned to Marr, who was in a struggle for second place.

"Is there anything I can do for you here, Dave?" he asked.

"Yeah," said the whimsical Marr. "Take a 12."

Though Palmer hasn't won since, he has persisted in his challenge. Nobody was close to Jack Nicklaus in 1965, but Palmer was as close as anybody else. He and Player tied in second place. His 290 was second low in 1966 when Nicklaus, Tommy Jacobs, and Gay Brewer indulged in another three-man play-off, and Nicklaus became the first successful defending champion. Palmer charged back into the group up front with a 69 on Sunday in 1967. He was still charging in 1975 and tied for second when the Saturday pairing threw him in with Nicklaus. Palmer shot himself out of it with a 75.

Whatever turns history may take, whatever interpolation may be written into it, no matter how many Masters Jack Nicklaus or some unknown player yet to arrive among us may win, there is no question that Arnold Palmer carried on the second "affair" with the late Baron Prosper J. A. Berckmans' acreage.

The first romance, of course, was Bobby Jones'.

...Back to the Drawing Board

"Everybody taking a mulligan here?"

The humor in it grabs at you only because the voice is Arnold Palmer's. A *mulligan* falls somewhere in Duffer's Laws of Procedure, a provisional second shot customarily allowed on the 1st tee — but, Arnold Palmer calling on a mulligan? This crutch reserved for 18-handicappers, flailers, slashers, lurchers, and company clients?

His first drive has hooked into the woods that form the elbow of the dogleg. He lashes into his mulligan, the ball takes an Arnold Palmer flight, with a most delicate touch of a draw, and makes an arc that follows the turn of the fairway, coming to rest about 265 yards away.

This scene and the steel mills and frigid winters of Pennsylvania, where Palmer grew his roots, are at opposite poles of American society. Bay Hill Club and Lodge is a jewel in a luxury setting, surrounded by the mushrooming affluence of central Florida. The specific area bears the name of Dr. Phillips, Florida, for a pioneer in the field of juices and citrus. Groves are everywhere, oranges and grapefruit hanging plump from limbs. Disney World is just across the lakes and through the trees. Jets from Orlando Jetport streak low overhead, making their descent for landing.

Bay Hill is all his now, the fruition of an ambition he'd pledged to himself the first time he saw Florida with the Wake Forest golf team in 1948. Oranges, right out in the open air. He'd never seen such a thing.

He has just finished closing the deal that made him proprietor of Bay Hill. The colors on the stone nameplate at the entrance are gold and black, those of Wake Forest's athletic teams. A pure coincidence. The sign was there before Palmer. The congestion in the parking lot indicates that business is good. A little crowd earlier had clustered about one section of the practice tee, where the proprietor was warming up for his afternoon game. It's a rare treat when a member can walk out on his own course and enjoy a free exhibition of Arnold Palmer striking golf balls. The formal fee is $12,500.

As soon as the Christmas traditions of Latrobe have been served, Palmer can be found at Bay Hill tuning up his game for the winter tour. He has played the first tournament of the season at Tucson and, failing to make the cut, has returned to base unhappy with himself, intent on relocating the old trim.

Conversation will not be hobbled by any degree of order, bobbing about from one reminiscence to another, weaving in and out of the Masters fabric, as he and his guest travel the front nine on the new demonstrator cart with his foursome, consisting of a friend who operates a farm; a retired golf professional who came to Florida having six months to live and here it is 30 years later; and a dentist. Palmer plays, his guest chauffeurs him.

"When I think about the Masters," he says, "I think about so many things. Amen Corner, where it's lost; and Nos. 16, 17, and 18, where it's won; the Masters Dinner on Tuesday night, and the frank conversation — sometimes too frank. 'Arnie's Army'— that's where it began, you know. I remember seeing it the first time on the scoreboard as I walked down the 11th fairway on Sunday in 1960. Somebody got a little too enthusiastic. They made them take it down. The way it got started, it had something to do with the soldiers from Fort Gordon marshalling that year.

"There's no doubt that the Masters established me. I'd won other tournaments, but when I won in 1958, that set me on the right track. It took away that cockiness and replaced it with confidence, if you know what I mean."

His second shot lands about 30 feet from the green. It is a par-five hole.

"It's one thing to be cocky and tell everybody how good you can play, and it's another thing to do it. I felt after winning in 1958 they knew how good I was. They'd seen it."

He pitches up four feet from the pin and sinks the putt for a birdie.

"Another thing about Augusta — even though I won it four times, I think of how I should have won it a lot more. '61, I hit it in the right bunker on No. 18 and knock it out across the green and take a 6. I wasn't cautious enough with the trap shot. I was trying to make 4 to win. '59, I knock it in the water and take 6 on No. 12."

Par three, 230 yards. He takes a two-iron and leaves himself about a 35-foot putt. He is not happy with it.

"'64, well, that one was the one I was looking for. That was the year I had quit smoking on January first. I finally broke down after about nine months, but I played the whole Masters without a cigaret. Never even thought about it.

"I'd always held the Masters in great awe. The concept, the way it was handled, I'd always kind of resented the complaints about this guy and that guy not being in the field. It's there for you if you can play. If you can play, you've got the same chance everybody else has to qualify."

He two-putts for his par.

"I'd always wanted to win one big. Leave no questions to be asked. To win and win decisively was important to me. I led all the way, from the 1st hole to the 72nd. That was the year I started out to set a new record on the last day, but it fizzled out. Then I came to the point that I thought, 'Well, you've got good position. Let's not blow the whole thing

trying for a record, and I just tried to hold my place the rest of the way. I won by six, and in my mind, I was pretty comfortable through the whole tournament."

He knocks a huge drive over the corner of a lake on the next hole, a par four. He laughs lightly, mood or memory, or both, who knows?

"The first time I tried to get to the Masters, I didn't make it. I wrote a letter volunteering the Wake Forest golf team as marshals. I was the coach. Bet you didn't know that, did you? That I coached the Wake Forest golf team? I'd been away in the Coast Guard, and when I came back they made me a sort of a coach. Anyway, they didn't take me up on my offer at Augusta National. It was a disappointment to me, now that I think about it."

His approach leaves him short. The wind grabs at it. He gets down in two for par.

"The first time I played in the Masters, I came in a trailer. Winnie and I had pulled that trailer all the way across the United States following the tour. We put it in a trailer park on U.S. 1 and lived in it during the tournament. After Augusta, we drove it home and parked it, and that was the last of that."

He is driving like the "Army's" Arnie. From the championship tee, 25 yards back of his companions, he lays the next tee shot out down the pike far in front of them all.

"We stayed at the Richmond Hotel after that for several years, until we thought we could finally afford a house. One year Dow and Linda Finsterwald and Winnie and I rented a house together, and it turned out to be the year we both wound up in a play-off with Player. Dow shot himself out of it pretty soon, and when we were walking to the 10th tee, he started giving me a pep talk. Dow and I were very close. Player was leading me by three strokes.

"'Come on,' he said, 'if I can't win it, you've got to. Keep it in the house.'"

Still another approach comes up short, 30 feet or more. His six-iron shot has stalled in the wind and died, but he two-putts for his par. Giving strokes, though, he and the dentist are down.

"Winning in '58 was some kind of experience, not just because it was my first, but because of the way it happened on the 12th hole. It was a traumatic experience because of my feeling for the Masters and how hard I was trying to win. I don't like to talk about it because I don't want to embarrass anybody. I read somewhere that I was throwing my arms around like Leo Durocher arguing with an umpire, and I did get pretty excited. My tee shot was imbedded between the green and the back trap. They'd handed us a rule at the 1st tee, and it said that the imbedded ball rule was in effect because the course was so soggy from all the rain we'd had.

"I played the imbedded ball, then dropped and played a provisional. The difference was two strokes. The worst thing about it was, I didn't get a ruling until the 14th hole when the committee sent somebody out from the clubhouse. It made winning that tournament as hard as anything I've ever experienced, but after winning, the way it happened made it all the better."

Another booming drive on the next hole, a crescent-shaped par five that fits around the other side of the lake, a two-iron across the lake, not crisply struck, but enough to roll the ball onto the green in two.

"The '62 tournament was a weird one for me. That's the one I won, lost, and won back again. I started out 70-66-69 and I go out Sunday two strokes up on Finsterwald. I came into the 16th hole two strokes out of the lead and finished 2-3-4. I realized I had to do something or I was dead. I hit my tee shot over the green on No. 16, a four-iron. Too much club. The adrenalin was really going.

"The ball was above the hole. Had a

good lie, but it was downhill, about 25 or 30 feet. I couldn't pitch it to the green. All I could do was get it started. Jimmy Demaret was working in the television booth, and I heard later that he said, 'There's no way for him to get down in two from there.' When it started rolling, I knew it was going to be close to the hole, rolling slow and smooth, and all of a sudden, in the hole. Then I knocked it close on No. 17 and got my birdie, and I was in the play-off."

His eagle putt just slides by the hole and he taps in for his second birdie. Now he is two under par.

"The next day I came out and played just awful on the front nine. I had a 38 and was three down to Player. Finsterwald, as I said, had already shot himself out of it. Then I birdied No. 10. I birdied the 12th — almost knocked it in for a 1. Birdied the 13th and 14th, and by the time we finished, I was three up on Gary. But here I was playing a fifth day in a tournament I should have won on Sunday."

The next hole is a par three, over a swale to a hill where the green sits. He hooks his tee shot and it makes the left side of the green, but he's left himself a monster of an uphill putt.

"If I ever have a golf tournament of my own, and it's anywhere nearly as successful as the Masters, I'm going to have a club of the champions, like the Masters Club. I've always thought the Masters Club was one of the great things about the tournament, one of the great traditions, and I look forward to it.

"The defending champion picks up the check and selects the menu. Clifford Roberts tells him what's available, and it's usually a steak of some kind, and always the pears or the peaches, Cliff's favorite little things. But that's part of the tradition, too.

"It has its constructive side, too. Oh, Harmon has his thing going, Demaret is cracking his jokes, and Snead always tells his X-rated stories. But some very constructive criticism comes out of it. Nicklaus is still the youngest member of the club. We were talking about that last year and that we were going to try to keep it that way. That can't last forever, of course. Some of the young fellows are bound to come on and win it. I look for Tom Watson to win it. Johnny Miller is a cinch to win it some day. Lee Trevino may even win it yet. Tom Weiskopf may never win it. You finish second as many times as he has, and you begin to develop a complex against winning it. It takes a special kind of player and attitude to win at Augusta."

He leaves the uphill putt short and commits the mortal sin of the pro — he three-putts on the par-three green. No. 8 at Bay Hill is a cuddlesome par four, 390 yards from the tournament tee. Palmer goes to the attack here, grits his teeth, sets his legs like pylons, surges into the ball with monstrous force, giving it that old finish that arouses his worshippers, club head high in the air above his grey brown hair blowing in the breeze. The ball almost disappears over the hill, leaving him just a pitch over a little pond to the green.

"Anytime the Masters comes up, you naturally think back to Bobby Jones. After Cliff Roberts introduced us, I used to have lots of talks with him, mainly about golf and the philosophy of it, the way the game was going and all that. Knowing him made a deep impression on me. I'd read his instructional book *Down The Fairway* when I was in high school, and it was the first golf book I ever read from cover to cover. Now I collect them."

The wind is coming up again and grabs at Palmer's approach. It is exasperating. The putt is another 30-yarder. Another par. He goes to No. 9 one under.

"Has it been frustrating, playing the Masters since '64? I've got to say I've enjoyed it all through those years, but I haven't enjoyed it as much as if I'd been winning. I've had to recognize the fact that I'm not going to win forever like I was winning there for a while. On the other hand, I go back each year with the thought that I may have it together one more time and win again. If I must confess it, I still have high hopes of winning it again.

"I think when it becomes absolutely hopeless, I'll quit playing. I don't think, right now, that I'd enjoy playing in it until I'm in my 60s or they have to gently suggest that I don't play any more. If I do play that long, the Masters would be the only tournament I'd play. It's the tournament of the world. I held it in awe when I was young, as I held the game of golf in awe, and I hold it in awe now. I still get that little tingle in my system when I turn down Magnolia Lane and begin the drive toward the clubhouse. There's really no other feeling like it in golf."

The ninth hole adds little to his introspection. A sturdy drive, an approach this time past the pin, down in two putts for a routine par. He's turned the front nine in 35 strokes, one less than par.

He stops for a hotdog with half a bun, which with mustard and relish requires a masterful handling touch. It is time to cut out, leave the game to the man who isn't satisfied yet to live on what he has accomplished, but looks ahead, when the taste of another victory would be as sweet as the first kiss. As the car pulls out of the driveway, this memory comes to mind of a line from a letter he once wrote the Augusta National hierarchy after he'd won the second time: "Even today I retain a longing to win it again and again."

It is a desire he has refueled each spring and which hasn't yet run out of timeliness. It is the Arnold Palmer that American hero worshippers love and clamor for. Forty-six years old and still charging.

Above: Charles Coody of Texas waves his cap and acknowledges gallery applause after sinking a putt in 1969, the year his challenge sank in the waters of the 15th hole. He redeemed himself in 1971.

Above right: Californian Billy Casper hits tee shot on 4th hole in 1970, the year he beat Gene Littler in a play-off.

Right: The scenic Argentine, Roberto de Vicenzo, sits unknowing for this portrait that reflects some of his despair of 1968.

Above: Gay Brewer, the Kentuckian who won in 1967 after losing in a play-off in 1966, strikes an approach shot.

Far left: Jack Nicklaus helps Tommy Aaron into green jacket in 1973, a rich moment in life for a boy only 125 miles from home.

Left: Art Wall made a stirring stretch drive of five birdies in the final six holes, closing out Arnold Palmer in 1959, then, disabled by an infection, became the only champion unable to defend his title. Here he hits a drive in 1974.

Bob Goalby…in the Company of the Great

Sam Snead (L) and Doug Ford (C) stand by as Bob Goalby,
Masters champion of 1968, hits his drive on 7th tee.

"You win all the Tucsons, all the Kempers, all the Insurance City Opens you can, nobody remembers. You win a Masters, nobody ever forgets."—Bob Goalby

On the uphill side of the finishing hole in those times sat a metal table, the kind you see at a beach, with only an umbrella to protect the occupants from the weather and distractions. Gathered about were officials, usually some person wearing one of the sacred green jackets and someone from the U.S.G.A. They were the accountants who accepted the scorecards of the players as they finished their rounds. Since that year, 1968, they have been moved inside the shelter of a tent.

It was a staggering year in many respects, 1968, covering a broad range of fascinations and discouragements. The stoutly brisk Mexican-American, Lee Trevino, made his emergence from the dungeons of poverty and played in the Masters. Tony Jacklin, son of a truck driver in Scunthrope, England, also made his first appearance. Bruce Devlin, barely eluding the career of plumbing in Australia, was tooling along with exceptional brilliance until he knocked his ball into the waters of the 11th hole and used eight strokes before finally extricating himself from its vise. Claude Harmon, full of surprises once every 20 years, startled the dead as well as the living when he knocked in holes in one consecutively in the course of the Par-Three tournament held Wednesday. He was hailed into the press building for the first time since he had won the Masters even more surprisingly in 1948. The unofficial "Big Three" were locked out. Arnold Palmer failed to make the cut. Gary Player held the lead twice, then was blown out. Jack Nicklaus shot a 67 in the fourth round and people were passing him.

The round of Sunday golf was something out of character for Augusta National. The proud old course was left in tatters, shot down in cold blood. It began with Player leading. He had used 210 strokes playing the first 54 holes. At least 10 players had a shot at the green coat, or made a run at it during the day, pleasantly perfect from the dawn to the dusk. There were 10 rounds under 70. "Possibly 1968 offered the most favorable weather conditions of all," Clifford Roberts wrote in his tournament summation.

It came to a close with all the excitement of a gold rush and a kind of confusion that only a tournament of the supreme composure of the Masters could absorb. You think of it as happening in the Quad-Cities Open or the Disney World Classic, the North and South Amateur or the Hope of Tomorrow tournament — not the Masters. No 45-year-old man — it was also his birthday — who had won 140 tournaments at every doglegged corner of the globe could possibly make such an oversight as to sign a card testifying to the accuracy of his own score when close perusal would have revealed a one-stroke improvement.

Central figure in this luckless drama was Roberto de Vicenzo, who plays magnificently but speaks in fractured English, as when he depicted his plight with this tragicomic phrase, "What a stupid!"

His nose is bulbous. His hair remains only in wispy strands. His appearance is more average middle-aged American until his generously Spanish-flavored dialect comes flowing forth, transferring the image to that of a movie gaucho. De Vicenzo began the final round at 212, two twosomes in front of Bob Goalby at 211. He was being joyously received by the gallery at the 18th green as a probable winner when he holed out and went to the scorer's table. There to attest into fact the horrible error.

Tommy Aaron, the native Georgian, had mistakenly written "4" in the square for the 17th hole when actually de Vicenzo had scored a 3. De Vicenzo signed it. "I am so happy, I see nothing but figures. I sign card and give it to official," he said later.

The rules of golf are universal and specific. In the code of the United States Golf Association, which maintains custody of the game in this country, it is written:

"The competitor is solely responsible for the correctness of the score recorded for each hole. . . . If the competitor returns a score for any hole lower than actually played, he shall be disqualified. A score higher than actually played must stand as returned."

The attesting line at the bottom of the Masters scorecard reads: "I have checked my score hole by hole." Beneath, Roberto de Vicenzo had signed his name. Instead of a 65, he assigned himself a 66. "Soon as you finish," one of the officials said with Augusta National propriety, "please come with me." Inside the headquarters building de Vicenzo, crushed and pathetic, had his error explained to him. Meanwhile on the course, Bob Goalby was playing toward home and a round of 66 that earned him the championship, though not assured, really, until he himself had reached the scorer's table.

Spectators, milling about with that dazed and directionless manner that comes from not knowing, were stunned as the news swept through by word of mouth. Nothing was official until the personages took their places for the awarding ceremony on the putting green. De Vicenzo sat dejectedly by, his face like a collapsed soufflé, while eulogies to his disaster were passed out, and Goalby was being green coated. It was not, at the moment, a popular twist of events, a fact made more pronounced when the pitiable de Vicenzo dolefully assayed his plight. "I am too old to do it again," he said.

Admirably, he exonerated Aaron. "Is my fault. I play too many rounds and sign too many cards all over the world. I know I have to look. From the start everything is right. [Using a nine-iron, he knocked his second shot in the cup for an eagle on the 1st hole.] Until 18th hole. Then I hit a hook. [It cost a bogey where a par would have overcome his careless arithmetic.] And sign wrong scorecard."

Almost obliterated in the outflow of empathy with the unfortunate and appealing visitor from the Argentine was the winner, Goalby. Piously patient, he stood by as a small boy who had been told he should be seen and not heard. For quite some time there was question that it would be the Masters recognized as lost by de Vicenzo rather than won by Goalby. When returned to cold reality, one first realized that had the error not been made, de Vicenzo would only have tied for the lead and would have been required to put down Goalby in a play-off Monday. Second, that at 277, Goalby had scored the third lowest 72 holes in all the Masters. Also, as time edged forward, Goalby conducted himself with such dignity that he became accepted as the winner of the Masters, 1968. Now the world views him with the respect that goes with the title.

... On Location

"Of course, mine was not like the others. It had a taint on it, but that wore off after a while."

Bob Goalby and friends walk down the 4th fairway at Medinah Country Club, about 25 or 30 miles west of Chicago, in the placid greenery of northern Illinois. A thunderstorm, with jagged bolts of lightning, soon will drive us to cover during this final practice round before the U.S. Open of 1975.

"Nobody seems even to remember that now. I have no asterisk by my name. Wherever I go, they introduce me as a winner of the Masters. It was a little painful at first. Everywhere I went there were questions. Sportswriters and broadcasters looked me up. The way it came out, I'd backed into the Masters. It still hadn't sunk in that Roberto still would have had to beat me in a play-off. Also, they hadn't looked back over the record of the Sunday round and realized that I had caught Roberto on the back nine after he had led the tournament at one time by two strokes.

"Anything I said of it then sounded defensive. It's all washed out with time. I feel as much at home in a green coat now as any winner on the grounds. It changed my life-style, especially in Augusta. Now they make room reservations for me, arrange tickets for me, meet me at the airport. They know who I am at the Club. I'm a Masters winner. If for nothing else but the Champions Dinner on Tuesday night alone, winning it was worth that.

"You win all the Tucsons, all the Kempers, all the Insurance City Opens you can, nobody remembers. You win a Masters, nobody ever forgets. I don't think you can say that about even the U.S. Open.

"Another thing that pleases me, look at the names of the other winners — Nicklaus, Snead, Nelson, Palmer, Hogan, Demaret, Player, and Smith. They've won the majority of them. There've been just a few of us like Aaron, Coody, Keiser, Harmon, Archer, and myself, the nongreat. Having your name up there with the great ones puts a premium on it."

He is playing with one of the great ones at this time. Their relationship is almost directly attributable to the Masters, their evenings at the Champions Dinners, and Goalby's unabashed respect for Sam Snead, by now a man 63 years old. ("Look at that swing," he says, as Snead lifts a shot with an iron off the 5th fairway, crisply and soundly struck. "Even at his age he still has the most fluid stroke of the ball in golf. Sam's a good fellow, too.") They are putting the last touches on their game for the U.S. Open championship which will begin the next day, and in which they will endure four rounds of rain, fiercely intolerant weather, and mud, black and gummy.

"What made the taste a little sweeter was that I'd never really played well at Augusta. I'd only broken 70 once. I'd never finished in the top 24 in seven years there. I shot a 66 and a 67 in practice and began to feel a little better about things. Then I took the early lead with a 70 in the first round, and I felt 'in the tournament' all the rest of the way.

"Funny thing, the way the thing ended. I was on the 15th green putting out an eagle while Roberto was putting out a birdie on 17. Both galleries let go at the same time. I was in the middle of the 17th fairway when I heard about his bogey on the 18th. Then I hit a poor approach and three-putted for a bogey there. I knew I had to have a par to tie on 18, and I played the hole with the pressure on. I didn't waltz in knowing I had a gift waiting for me. I sliced my drive into the woods, and it hit something and bounced back out on the fairway. That left me a long second shot. I asked for my two-iron and hit a career shot about 220 yards to the green, got down with two putts, and the next thing I seem to realize, I was having my arms slipped into the finest shade of green jacket I ever wore."

Always the family man, never quite at ease with the constant demand of a life that uprooted him and sentenced him to long periods in aircraft cabins and alone in motel rooms, the Masters had opened new alternatives to Goalby. At this very moment he is enjoying the familial pleasure of watching his nephew move in to pick up and carry on the blood heritage.

His name is Jay Haas, Goalby's sister's child, another member of the day's foursome. It will be a radiant June for Jay Haas, who will tie for low amateur in the Open, then move on to Columbus, Ohio, and capture the National Collegiate Championship the next week. It gives Goalby a sense of relief to know that he will not lose totally his contact with and interest in the tournament tour.

Across the blacktop road from the 12th hole an angry storm is astew over the amusement park, where the shrill sounds arise of children squealing with contentment and fear briefly endured.

"My days on the tour are about over. I'm checking in as teaching pro at a new club in Palm Springs, a kind of settled life I've always wanted for my family. I've got a 12-year-old son I've never played golf with. It's a job I wouldn't have if I hadn't won the Masters. Now I can go back forever. Teeing off at the Masters is like when they play the national anthem to me. Even after you've won it, that tingly feeling doesn't go away when they announce your name, and you step up to hit your shot on the 1st tee."

As the teeing area of the 17th hole is approached — the excruciating 17th where, ironically, Sam Snead had lost the 1948 Open to Cary Middlecoff — the fury catches up with us and breaks loose upon us. Wind, terrifying bolts of lightning, followed by thunder that jars the earth like a quake, and then rain coming down by the bucketful. Snead's caddy, a young chap not accustomed to such an illustrious client, has forgotten the umbrella. Goalby shares his, and there they stand, two winners of the Masters huddled under one umbrella. The scene shrinks from the view of the wiser galleryites who flee for the clubhouse and shelter, turning, though, for a last glance over their shoulders at Sam Snead and one of the "non-great."

Jack Nicklaus sandblasts to the 2nd green, ball flying toward the flag, his gallery ringed behind him on the hillside and among the trees.

On the picturesque 13th green Jack Nicklaus sags
as a putt misses its mark.

One of the largest of Augusta National's greens, the 6th, and one of the smallest of the Masters' champions, Gary Player of South Africa.

Jack Nicklaus, trimmed down and coiffured, "after he got pretty," as one of his sons described it, eye to eye with . . .

While Johnny Miller's putt rolls by the hole on the 18th green, Tom Weiskopf waits his turn in one of the Masters' most dramatic finishes in 1975. Both missed, and with each miss went a chance for a tie with Jack Nicklaus.

...Arnold Palmer, his charm and male appeal etched in his face.

Jack Nicklaus. . .His Time Is Now

Jack Nicklaus grimly lines up a putt on the 15th hole in the final round of 1975 as
the battle tightened. His birdie attempt failed.

"What other knights are there left to joust, windmills left to tilt?"
"To win it six, seven, and eight times."— Jack Nicklaus

Jack Nicklaus came to Augusta National a fat kid with a porcupine haircut and no use for a tailor. He bulged beneath his clothing. He had a Teutonic countenance, that cold kind of tempered fierceness at gaming that could victimize with a smile. He was a boy installed in a man's body with a man's muscles, playing a man's game, and years ahead of schedule for one cherub-cheeked and only 19.

He came as an amateur that first time, a spring quarter dropout from Ohio State University having his first run of eminence in the Great Big Golf World out there. His qualification was as a member of the Walker Cup team, the best of the nonprofessionals who defend national honor against England's best.

Now, 17 Masters later, the depiction is that of a giant thundering across the acres of pines and flowering shrubs, footsteps resounding through the forest. A Gulliver taking Brobdingnagian strides among players he dwarfs. This is a different, more scenic Jack Nicklaus now. Svelte, trimmed to male model athlete proportions. Well-tailored, to the country club and tournament taste. Blond hair grown long, dripping carelessly over his forehead, hanging loosely about the nape of his neck. He had taken serious steps to rid himself of that bulging, fat boy image. Flying home from the Ryder Cup matches in England in 1969, he'd taken the vow. He'd gone on a severe diet, and the next time the public got a close-up of him, they saw not a totally unsimilar re-run of the fairy tale of the frog that became a prince. He was stunning. The world became his people. It began to look him up and learned to idolize instead of be chafed by him.

It had been conceded as inevitable that he would sometime take charge of this golf tournament as if this very land were his. The public had become impatient with him when he did not become the first amateur to win it. But once he became a professional, the wait was short. Guldahl, Wood, Snead, Hogan, Middlecoff, and Casper had to serve time until they were on the mellowing side of their 30s before they won the Masters, but Nicklaus was being fitted out in his first green jacket at the bumptious age of 23. When you consider that he only arrived in Augusta in 1959, and that he began playing professionally only in 1962, and that by 1975 he had already won the Masters five times, you are qualified then to cower before the awesomeness of his impact on not simply one tournament, but global golf.

He walked into the teeth of the storm, literally, in 1963 and with a doggedness and a response to pressure considerably beyond that expected of a yearling in a field of thoroughbreds came forth the winner. While older and more seasoned players were knuckling under to the horrid conditions produced by a constant rain in the third round, he stiff-upper-lipped it and played himself into the lead with a score of 74. No one within shooting distance of the lead broke 70 that day. He won it, lost it, and won it back on Sunday when Sam Snead, then 51, suffered a disastrous collapse and bogeyed in. Out on the course Nicklaus got the news that he had to par home from the 17th to beat Tony Lema, who had stroked in a twisting putt on No. 18 to take the clubhouse lead. He held his calm and did it.

Thus was the Nicklaus Era of the Masters sworn in. When he won it again in 1965 — a year the Dodgers were winning the World Championship of baseball, our military in Vietnam was digging itself a trench for the most unpopular war ever fought, and we were up to our scalps in the hairiness of the Hippie Generation — and then repeated in 1966, it seemed the Masters might be in a vise-like grip from which only the process of aging could release it. The most overpowering golfer of the age was upon us. No one could see another player in the daily PGA lineup who might possibly ever beat Jack Nicklaus again at Augusta. He had staked his claim.

True, luck had done a dance for him in 1966. The dour Kentuckian, Gay Brewer, had only to sink a seven-foot putt on the 18th green on Sunday to make the green jacket his, but the thing slid by the hole. Nicklaus was granted a reprieve along with a smooth-swinging but seldom-winning California professional, Tommy Jacobs. Nicklaus took no prisoners in the Monday play-off. He wiped them out.

But just as certain immortality was his, mortality overcame him in 1967. He suffered the worst round he has ever played at Augusta. A 79 sent him awinding and out of the tournament two days early. Gritting his teeth and swallowing his pride, he sportingly, though grimly, followed some of the action of the third round from a cart with Clifford Roberts before fleeing. Then Sunday at dusk he had to suffer through the ordeal at the presentation ceremony of holding the green coat for Brewer, the new champion, to slip into.

Whatever effect this crushing experience had on him, it is a matter of record that it was five years before he won again, during which time he managed to come close only in 1971, the Charlie Coody year.

The Nicklaus Era was back in office again the following spring and with the rap of authority. He took the lead the first day and never lost it until he was safely inside a green jacket again. He was the only player who broke par for 72 holes. He became Arnold Palmer's companion as the only four-time winners. No pressing effort was required of him in round four, when he shot a clubby 74 in a great wind, never felt any heat, and won by three strokes over Bruce Crampton, the Americanized Australian, and Bobby Mitchell, muffin-faced North Carolinian.

1974 was but a hyphen year in his Masters record. Though he started and finished with 69s, he lost to his close friend Gary Player by three strokes. 1975 was his again, and now for six years in a row he has never been below fourth place. But '75 was the year of the smashing finish. Boffo! as in the entertainment vocabulary. Nicklaus, Tom Weiskopf, and Johnny Miller in a bell-ringer down the backside nine. First one in the lead, then the other.

"The writer," being Clifford Roberts, founder, chairman, historian, and the Masters himself, "cannot recall a single instance when three contestants of such recognized ability stayed so close together during the finishing holes; when all three played so well during the last round; and when the winner could not be determined until all three had putted out on No. 18. Neither Weiskopf nor Miller lost the tournament. Jack Nicklaus won it." This Roberts wrote in his annual final minutes of the meeting.

Actually, Nicklaus sat before dark television cameras in the ceremonial room of Butler Cottage while Miller and Weiskopf both missed makeable putts on the 18th green that would have tied him. It was a great game. It sloshed with drama. Every green became a new stage. It was hours before the tide of adjectives subsided in the press building. It was great theater. It was fun. Jack Nicklaus himself confirms that.

So he stands the monarch of Augusta. A giant in a green coat. Only winner of

five Masters. Lowest in scoring average per round. Tied for the lowest round of 64. Holder of the record for 72 holes (a record Ray Floyd tied in '76), when in 1965 he left the course in ruins, removing 17 strokes from par; also winner by the suppressive margin of nine strokes, a record. Winner of the most prize money, or an average of $51 per stroke. And the most feared rival the 18 holes of Augusta National have had. The one of whom, while he's still on the course, all the other players now ask, "What's Jack doing?"

This is remindful of a story Gene Sarazen once told in a verbal essay on Bobby Jones, and the finest compliment, the Squire thought, that could ever be paid a player. "Whatever tournament he was playing, wherever it may have been, everybody always asked, 'What's Bobby doing?'"

. . .In the Executive Suite

Here is a man still too young for nostalgia. His memories are Now. He's living his memories. He's still the youngest guest at the annual Champions Dinner. He has had his peaks and his valleys, his high rides and his slumps, but fewer valleys and fewer slumps than the average immortal. Still, the question seems urgent, at least essential. It is one of those general questions that interviewers ask, but with a very definite aim in mind: Of the five Masters Jack Nicklaus has won, which does he cradle most lovingly among his affections?

"I'd have to mention two," he says, "1965 and 1975. The Masters of '75 was the most fun golf tournament I've ever played in. I never had so much fun playing golf. I loved it. It finished like it was supposed to, the three players who had been having the best year, Weiskopf, Miller, and me, coming down to the wire. Everybody playing good golf. Nobody

Jack Nicklaus putts on the 13th green, a hole on which he is considerably below par for his Masters career.

choking."

"That was exciting. It was fun, that's what it was."

Driving north on U.S. 1, Main street of America's East Coast, you see a bridge over the Intracoastal Waterway at North Palm Beach, and on the right just across that bridge, a cluster of buildings in the typical architecture of the '70s development vintage springs up amid palms and waterways into air washed by the surf. Old Port Cove is a combination of living and business, condominium and office unit.

"Golden Bear Ent." is listed unpretentiously among the shops, the brokers, the realtors, and the manufacturers' reps who run their business out of these prefabricated hutches connected by walkways. All that's needed to identify the Nicklaus operational center is the insignia, a gold bear. Inside the reception room are pictures of him swinging his MacGregor golf clubs and tennis racquets, modeling his Hathaway shirts and his Hart, Schaffner & Marx suits, driving his Pontiac cars and riding on his Firestone tires. And these are but a few of the products that keep wheels and executives turning. They grovel for his endorsement. Business is booming. And on the wall, displayed prominently, is the reason — or reasons, for there are 16 of them: a roll call of the 16 major golf tournaments he has won brought up to date through the PGA championship of 1975.

A mounted sailfish is suspended across one wall, a taxidermied victim of another of his talents. He has only recently returned from winning the Australian Open, followed by a week pursuing the wild game of the deep off Australia's shores. Then followed up, on his return home, by a weekend in Columbus, where he flew his three sons to watch Archie Griffin, of Heisman Award acclaim, play his final game in Ohio Stadium and to see Ohio State defeat Minnesota.

His dress is quite casual — green shorts, brown shirt, and sneakers. "Florida executive business suit," he calls it. His office is man-sized but uncluttered, with one of those desks as big as a steamship at which he spends little of his time. Home is up the road a piece at Lost Tree Village, and when Jack Nicklaus is at home, Jack Nicklaus is *at home*. He will not play another round of golf for a month. His detachment from the game will be absolute until his return to the winter tournaments in the West.

"Whoever made the pairings in the third round created the fourth," he says, moving ahead on the Masters of 1975. "Arnold and I were not on the board to be paired Saturday. All other tournaments make their pairings dead by the numbers, which is the fairest way to do it. Augusta reserves the privilege of using its own discretion, and somebody wanted a Palmer-Nicklaus pairing. Anyway, it threw Arnold right out of the tournament. He was far more unhappy with the pairing than I was. I've played well with Arnold on many occasions, but he rarely plays well with me. We both got caught up in playing each other, as usual.

"The thing that brought all the excitement to a head on Sunday was when Tom Watson had all the trouble on the 16th. We were paired for the fourth round. While he stood there and knocked golf balls in the water, making his 8, I had watched Weiskopf and Miller play the 15th hole. So we've got all this tension building up. Watson playing himself out of the tournament. Weiskopf holing a long one on No. 15. They're coming to the 16th tee, and everybody's waiting for me to putt out on the 16th green. Uphill, 40 feet or maybe more. Really, it was the putt that made my whole year. It was probably the most exciting putt I ever made, in a crucial situation, in a major tournament. This one was totally unexpected, yet one when

I got over the ball, I had a feeling I was going to make.

"You know, there's not a more exciting place in the game of golf than the 16th hole at Augusta, with the crowd sitting there in that amphitheater, and the crucial way that the 15th and 16th come together there. It set up the year for me. It obviously won the tournament for me, and it came at a critical stage in my life when everybody was saying here comes Johnny Miller and Nicklaus is all washed up. Well, we squelched that for at least another year.

"1965, now that was fun of another kind. No matter what I did I made a birdie. I reduced the golf course to nothing that year. It was playing short, anyway, and the fairways were firm, and I made every putt I looked at. And won by nine strokes, 17 under par, which I didn't think was too bad."

America's children grow up with an acute awareness of ambition, an urgency, as well as the right, to succeed. They train their thought lines along being president, a firefighter, a policeman, or an all-American halfback or playing centerfield for the New York Yankees. This is the immediate range of their versions of the future. The doctor and the lawyer and the public accountant in them come out as maturity takes over. Jack Nicklaus grew up wanting to be the first amateur to win the Masters.

"The first Masters I ever really remember was in '54, with Billy Joe Patton, when so much was made of it because he was an amateur. Then Ken Venturi's year in '56. Being an amateur myself, it was always nice to see the amateurs do well and have a chance of winning, but I wanted to be first. Of course, I wasn't, but that became one of my goals about '56 when I saw Venturi almost do it on television.

"My first Masters was '59. I went down two weeks early. I'd made up my mind

that because of the two-week trip with the Walker Cup team in May and playing in the Masters, I'd drop out of school for the spring quarter. I gave up my first year of college golf for that. This was something I really wanted to do.

"I went down with a friend of mine from Ohio State. I didn't know about the rules at Augusta about bringing friends. You know, I was just a 19-year-old kid. We ran into an advertising executive from New York who befriended us, and we got to play golf every day we were there. Then after four days we got into the car and drove to Wilmington, North Carolina, and entered the Azalea Open. I was excited about the Masters and thought I could use a little tournament experience. I had a sponsor's exemption because of the Walker Cup team, and I played the first two rounds. Shot 73-74 and was in fourteenth place. But I wasn't happy with my play at all. I wasn't used to being in fourteenth place. So I left. I said, 'To heck with this, I'm going back to Augusta and practice.' Can you believe that?

"If I'd shot 70-70, I'd have won the tournament, but you got to remember, I'm this impetuous 19-year-old kid. I caught all sorts of hell from the PGA people. I didn't know any better. I'd played in a pro tournament only once before, and I thought when you didn't like the way things were going, you got out. So I went back to Augusta. That's how excited I was about playing in the Masters.

"I stayed in the clubhouse at Augusta National during tournament week, up in the 'crow's nest.' Tommy Aaron, Deane Beman, Ward Wettlaufer, Phil Rodgers, and myself, the young amateurs. They charged you a dollar for lunch and $2.50 for dinner, or something like that. I ate two shrimp cocktails and two New York strips every night.

"I shot 76-74 and I'll never forget; I'd

After missing a putt for a birdie on No. 15, Jack Nicklaus makes it up to himself on No. 16 as an uphill 40-footer finds the cup on Sunday, 1975. "Probably the most exciting putt of my career," he said.

never seen greens of that speed. Through 36 holes I'd hit 31 greens in regulation, three-putted eight times, and was out of the tournament. Palmer had hit 19 greens, shot 142, and was leading. I was three shots behind Art Wall, and he won the tournament. The thing that killed me was No. 12. I hit it in the water and made double bogey there, and it killed my chance of making the cut. But it was a heck of an experience for me. I stayed around the next two days and watched.

"I came back two more years as an amateur. I finished thirteenth in '60 and seventh in '61, and that was as close as I came to realizing my ambition of winning it as an amateur.

"One of the nicest things that has happened to me at Augusta was the turn-around from '63. You know, in '63 I was the little fat kid who came down invading Arnold's domain. I wasn't exactly the most popular golfer around. Here's a kid coming out of school and he's got that short haircut and he doesn't look any more like an athlete than Sonny Jurgenson. I remember one of those years I hit a ball to the 9th green, and it starts rolling back off the putting surface. People start clapping. It was one of the most embarrassing moments I've been through. Anyway, the turnaround has been nice.

"That was the tournament that Mike Souchak gave away, the '63 tournament. I played with Mike in the third round. He was leading, and I was a stroke behind. That was the day it rained like the devil, and a lot of the fairways were just casual water. I just kept playing and kept trying. I kept telling myself, 'They haven't called this thing off. We're still playing out here.' And Mike gave up. He must have shot a million. I shot 74, which was a good score that day. I didn't realize until I got to the 18th hole that I was leading. I'd been seeing all these '1's on the score-boards, but I'm color blind, and I couldn't

tell if they were green or red until we got close enough to the scoreboard at the 18th to tell the difference.

"I looked at my caddy and said, 'Willie, am I right? Am I the only red one up there?'

"'Yeah, boy, you sure are,' he said. I was leading the tournament and didn't know it until then. I shot 74-72 the last two rounds, and of course Tony Lema shot that great last round, but I won it, and there I was standing on the putting green with Arnold helping me get into one of those green jackets and Bob Jones congratulating me."

A telephone rings and his secretary says it is some fellow who needs to talk to him about a golf course in Spain. Nicklaus offers his consulting services around the world. One group of Japanese have paid him a fabulous fee to help them lay out the St. Andrews of the Orient.

"About Bob Jones, when I was growing up around Scioto Country Club in Columbus in the 1950s, about all I ever heard was 'Bob Jones, Bob Jones.' There were pictures of him on the walls and reminders of him all about the place. He'd won the U.S. Open there in 1926. In 1955, I qualified for my first National Amateur, and it was played in Richmond, Virginia. Bob Jones was there to be speaker at the banquet. The day of the last practice round he was out on the course, and he watched me hit my second shot to the 18th green, which was an old par-five hole converted into a par four at the James River Country Club. He asked somebody who I was and was told that I was the youngest player in the tourna-ment. He called me over.

"'Young man,' he said to me, 'I've been out here quite awhile, and you're the first person to reach this green in two.'

"That night at the banquet he talked to me for a few minutes and told me that he'd been impressed with what he'd seen at the 18th that afternoon. He said he was going to come out and watch me play some holes the next day.

"When he came out, I was leading Bob Gardner, one of the best amateurs in the country, one up. I proceeded to go bogey-bogey-double bogey while he watched. Then he left, and I evened the match but got beat on the 18th hole. He told me later that he left because he didn't think he was doing me much good. Well, that was my introduction to Bob Jones."

He wrestled with himself over the lure of professionalism some years later, did Nicklaus. There were values to be observed by remaining amateur, but would he ever know how good he might be if he did not take on the best golfers in the world at their own game? He balanced on the high wire of indecision until one day in November, 1961, he turned professional. In the mail that same day came a letter from Bob Jones, who had read of his agonizing and who appealed to him to resist the enticements of professionalism and to carry on carrying the banner of amateurism high.

Following his years of successive championships, Nicklaus endured one of the two darkest days of his career as a player — he didn't make the cut in the Masters of 1967, though two months later he was to break the scoring record for the U.S. Open at Baltusrol.

"The 79 on Friday was probably the most frustrating round of golf I've ever played. I didn't think I played all that badly. Only two or three times in my life have I had the putting yips. That was one of them. I kept leaving myself three-foot putts all day long and missing them. Another time was in the National Amateur in 1960. I'd beaten Phil Rodgers in the morning round, really zipped him, 7 and 6. That afternoon I was paired with a fellow named Lewis from Little Rock. Phil and I had a big rivalry going in those days, and after beating him, the tournament was over for me. I went out in the afternoon and three-putted six times on the front nine, once from three feet. Lewis beat me, 5 and 3 — just killed me. Charles Lewis from Little Rock, Arkansas. Never was heard from again. Well, I was having that kind of day at Augusta, and I've had only two of them since I've been playing golf.

"As a golf course, Augusta National isn't that tough. It is considered one of the great golf courses of the world because of its beauty, its traditions, what has happened there, and its place in golf. And Bob Jones. That's what's Augusta. It's a good golf course, but it isn't a great golf course. The public has made it so. With the public, the Masters is the greatest golf tournament in the world."

You win it five times, what other knights are there left to joust, windmills left to tilt? What challenge is left? What can possibly inspire a man who has done this to stalk forth upon the acreage in pursuit of another?

"That's easy," says Jack Nicklaus. "To win it six, seven, and eight times."

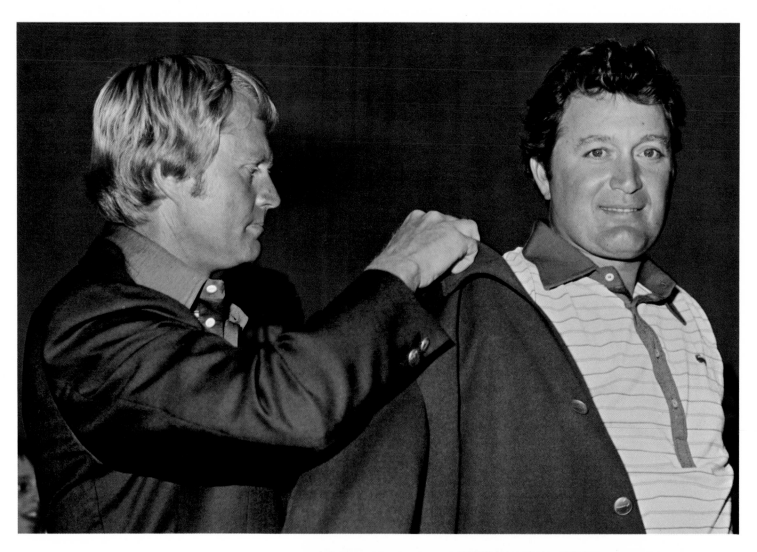

Above: Jack Nicklaus (L) puts the coat of one color – greatness – on 1976 Masters champion, Ray Floyd.

Right: Ken Venturi, the young recent Army corporal, surrounded by golf writers of America, at a table in the clubhouse before he went out on the Sunday round, 1956, to the most devastating day of his life.

Left: Gene Littler, purpose-fully on his way to a putt as his caddy prepares to hand him his weapon. He came close but lost in a play-off with Billy Casper in 1970.

Right: Billy Joe Patton, the daring amateur from North Carolina who almost beat Snead and Hogan in 1954, leaning on his driver.

Below: Dow Finsterwald, Gary Player, and Arnold Palmer (L to R) on the day of their play-off in 1962. Palmer won by three strokes, and there went Finsterwald's big chance.

Above: Peter Oosterhuis chipping. No other Britisher has come as close as he did in 1973.

Right: Tony Jacklin, another of Her Royal Majesty's subjects, blasting out of a bunker on the 2nd hole. He came from out of nowhere in 1968.

Above: Don January, the silent Texan, on the tee. His 66 on the final round missed catching George Archer by two in 1969.

Left: Takaaki Kono, the wee Japanese, watching the flight of a fairway shot on No. 1. He eagled the same hole in 1970, one of the four there in the history of the Masters.

They Also Played…the Near-Misses

Bert Yancey, who came frustratingly close three times, watches a shot
with a quizzical expression befitting the puzzle of his career in the Masters.

"The luck balances out. . . . the
putts will drop and I'll win one."
— Tom Weiskopf

In 1956 Ken Venturi, a most promising
amateur, was barely known beyond the
city limits of San Francisco. But he played
in the Masters tournament because he
had the right friends. One was Byron
Nelson, who, it seems, was responsible
for influencing the vote of former
Masters champions who in those days
were allowed to vote one player into the
field. The other was Ed Lowery, whose
greatest claim to sporting fame is that he
bagged for Francis Ouimet when Ouimet
became the first amateur winner of the
U.S. Open championship. Lowery was a
man of some clout among Augusta
National members.

He owned automobile dealerships in
San Francisco, and on his roster of
officers was the name of Venturi, a vice-
president, though the demand for 24-
year-old vice-presidents has always run
light, except for those with picturesque
golf swings and scratch handicaps. For
Venturi advancement had been swift. He
was only recently returned from
Germany, a few weeks removed from the
rank of corporal, U.S. Army.

His wife was a tall, lissome, sultry girl
of dramatic proportions. Conni Venturi,
in her time, became almost as well known
for her elegance as her husband for his
golfing ability. But she was not with Ken
on this trip. Being a poor amateur, he
could not have afforded the expense
anyway, but only a few days before she
had given birth to their first child.

The first time Venturi struck Augusta
National, the course was left dizzy and
reeling. He shot a 66 on the opening day
of the Masters, and that is still the lowest

score any amateur has ever made. He followed this with a 69 on a treacherously windy day on which Ben Hogan surrendered to a 78. Even a 75 on Saturday left Venturi still on top of the field by four strokes.

It had become custom since Bob Jones had retired from play that Byron Nelson as unofficial Club host be paired with the leader of the tournament on the Sunday round. Since Nelson had been Venturi's mentor, at Lowery's behest, and his sponsor, it was determined in tournament headquarters that it would not be proper to allow a pairing so favorable to Venturi. So Venturi was paired for the final round with Sam Snead, who does not smile at his playing companions a great deal, nor waste his time passing compliments. After they've teed off, Sam is a shop open only for business.

The wind was cranky again on Sunday with gusts up to 50 m.p.h. Greens had dried out until they crackled as putts rolled across them. It wasn't a good day for many players. Nelson himself shot an 80. Jimmy Demaret, three-time winner, shot 81, Lionel Hebert an 83, Fred Hawkins an 84. One professional shot 86.

Meanwhile, the course was extracting its pint of blood from the kid who had played fancy with its traditions for three days. Venturi came limping home in 80 strokes. He needed only a 40 on the back nine to win, but he bogeyed six holes and finished one stroke down to Jack Burke, Jr., who had shot a pleasant 71 and moved from eight behind and won with a score of 289, one above 72-hole par. Venturi was crushed. He came away from the 18th green and walked laboriously up the incline to the clubhouse lawn like a man sagging beneath a boulder. There he burst into tears.

But Sam Snead did not shoot Venturi's 80. Venturi himself asked to make that clear after these years of silence on the subject. "Do you know the reason I was paired with Sam?" asked Venturi. "I asked to play with him. They wouldn't let me play with Byron, which I thought was a fair decision as we were so close. So they gave me a choice. I had played with Hogan and with Demaret in earlier rounds, and I wanted to play the last round with another one of the greats. Sam didn't help me. He was not supposed to. He certainly did nothing to hurt me. I shot the 80."

This was the beginning of a non-romance between man and Masters. It seemed this ground was not meant for Venturi. Two years later, paired with Arnold Palmer on Sunday, he suffered through the distraction of the imbedded ball incident, not knowing if he led or didn't lead. He fell behind and lost by two strokes.

Venturi's final devastation came in 1960. Winning now almost certainly was assured — he could feel it in his bones. He had finished on Sunday with a round of 70 and a total score of 283. There was by this time an order of procedure at the Masters in which any seeming winner is met by a man in a green coat, a press committee member driving a green cart, as he leaves the 18th green. He is delivered to Clifford Roberts' private quarters, there to await the television presentation to the nation. It is here over television monitors that several potential winners of the Masters have sat and watched themselves shot out of the lead, dying by the inch and in soulful need of solace.

Arnold Palmer was the only person on the course with a chance to catch Venturi in 1960, and even Arnold the Charger, the Magnificent, the Adored, seemed hopelessly outmatched. He needed birdies on the last two holes. Palmer got them and as Palmer got them, Venturi sat and watched, sequestered and gutted, tears coming once again. Two times taunted and two times denied. He won the U.S. Open in 1964, almost a walking zombie in the unmerciful heat of Washington, D.C., and it was appreciated. Somewhere up there somebody cared. But it was not the one he wanted. The one he wanted never came. Ken Venturi, who might have been two times, never was a Masters champion.

Three years later, a close friend and contemporary of Venturi's made the same trip. Tony Lema, also of San Francisco, had gone into the Sunday round needing three strokes to catch the nice, young, fat kid from Ohio, Jack Nicklaus. When he turned the front nine in 35, one under par, he felt a surge of the electrical power of success. When he sank a twisting, downhill 22-foot putt for a birdie on the 18th green for another 35 on the back nine, he, too, was intercepted by the man in the green coat and taken to Roberts' private chambers.

There he was introduced to Bobby Jones for the first time, and while social calesthenics were farthest from his mind at the time, this formal introduction did sort of ease his tension. He was invited to have a seat and watch the finish on the monitor. He decided he'd wash his hands and comb his hair. Bowman Milligan, major domo of the Club and the man in charge of the green jackets, asked Lema for his size.

"I'm a 42 long," Lema said.

Lema came out of the bathroom just in time to see the most discouraging television show he ever watched — Jack Nicklaus reaching the 18th green and getting down in two strokes and closing him out. And Bowman could forget the size 42 long.

"All I could do was sit and watch," Lema wrote later in his book, *Golfer's Gold.* When that last putt dived out of sight and into the hole, so did all my emotions and hopes. I felt I would never have the strength to rise from the chair I was sitting in."

When it was all over and Lema was free to leave, he walked outside and found Venturi waiting for him. As boys they had caddied together. They had shared a house that week. More teardrops fell, and once again the Masters had struck close to where Ken Venturi kept his emotions filed.

Tony Lema later won the British Open, but later, too, a terrible tragedy struck him down. He died in a light private plane that crashed, strange as it may seem, on a golf course in Illinois.

None has had such a remarkable triumph as Claude Harmon, who stopped over on his annual migration from the pro shop at Seminole Golf Club in Florida to the pro shop at Winged Foot Golf Club in New York and won the Masters on his vacation in 1948. But many have been unrighteously struck down. Harry Cooper, Lloyd Mangrum, Dow Finsterwald, Gene Littler, Tom Weiskopf, and Bert Yancey, unflinching nomads of the tour all, were never, or haven't yet been, able to win a Masters — literally, tauntingly were turned away at the threshold of the championship. The story of "Lighthorse" Harry Cooper's experiences in the classic tournaments of golf was one of rejection. Twice it had seemed he had the U.S. Open championship in his lap, and twice it got away. Once at Oakmont, where Tommy Armour tied him with his last putt, then beat him in a play-off; the other time at Baltusrol, where it seemed he left no room for doubt when he set a record of 284 strokes, then endured the deflating experience of defeat by a club pro, Tony Manero, who lowered the record still two more strokes later in the same afternoon.

One year Cooper was the Vardon Trophy winner. Once he was the leading PGA money winner. Many times he won

Though fate was to cut Tony Lema down before his time, he made his impression on the 1963 Masters.

tour tournaments of prestige, the Los Angeles Open twice, for instance, but always the big one eluded him, just as the Masters did in 1936, a rugged year of tempestuous weather that forced the field to finish with 36 holes on Monday. Even then they very nearly finished under water. The course had been turned into a bog. Rain broke out again during the day. Casual water rules were in effect all about the course, one of these favoring Horton Smith, who got a 22-foot drop that allowed him to move his ball out of some mild rough onto the green at the 12th hole. So favored, Smith gathered steam the closer he came to the clubhouse, where Cooper sat, a fidgeting wreck, after finishing 71-76 — 286. He had begun the 36-hole day five strokes in the lead, and now as he waited, he listened to reports of Smith's chipping away at him until the lead was gone, and he had lost again by a stroke. It was then that Harry Cooper turned mournfully to Bob Jones and said, "It must not be intended for me to win a major tournament."

And he never did. This Texan from Chicago — actually, he was a naturalized native of England who had been reared in Texas — finished four strokes behind Jimmy Demaret in 1941 and kept returning to Augusta National until the intermission for World War II, after which he faded from sight.

Lloyd Mangrum fell upon the Masters like a sonic boom. The first time he played a round he unraveled the course record with a 64 in 1940. It was as substantial as it was astonishing, and it stood for 25 years, and then Jack Nicklaus could only tie it. Of course, Augusta National was not the same course that it is today, but a 64 is a 64 and shall remain a 64. Unfortunately, Mangrum didn't have another one in his bag and finished second to Demaret that year.

In 1949, Mangrum teed off Sunday tied for the lead with Sam Snead, but nobody was passing Sam that day. Mangrum took two strokes off par and still was beaten by three. He was third to Hogan in both of Hogan's winning years, two strokes out of Snead and Hogan's play-off in 1954, three strokes back of Jack Burke, Jr., in 1956 while Ken Venturi's lead was out there for anybody to grab, and it was then that Lloyd Mangrum's Masters contention came to a close.

Finsterwald's challenge took place in the early '60s, shortly after he had won the PGA championship. He was the third man in the play-off with Arnold Palmer and Gary Player in 1962; however, he could have muscled in on the year of Palmer's grand emergence in 1960 but for a slip of etiquette. On his way to a 71 in the Thursday round, Finsterwald had missed a short putt on the 5th green, dropped his ball, and made a practice putt in his unhappiness.

Paired with Bill Casper for the second round the next day, Finsterwald was about to repeat his faux pas as they started to leave the second green when Casper called to him.

"That'll get you a penalty, Dow," he said.

Pulling out the scorecard, Casper showed him the rule clearly stated on the back. Upon reaching the clubhouse after the round, Finsterwald turned himself in and was assessed a two-stroke penalty. Which in itself was a break, for the Tournament Committee could have disqualified him. As it turned out, Palmer won the tournament 282 to Finsterwald's 284. Those two strokes had been the difference.

Anticipation of Gene Littler winning a Masters is a bow to aesthetics. His swing is so smooth, so flawless that he is called "Gene the Machine." His four rounds of 69-70-70-70 in 1970 were just as consistent as Claude Harmon's in 1948, but not enough to win, only enough to tie Bill Casper. Casper then took him by five strokes in the play-off on Monday.

Beginning with 1967, Bert Yancey and Tom Weiskopf alternately endured an unwelcomed tenure as personal caretakers of the near-miss. Yancey, a former West Point cadet, reached Augusta National at the age of 28, and making his first appearance in 1967, played the course in 67 strokes on Thursday, three ahead of his nearest pursuers, Bill Casper and Downing Gray, an amateur from Pensacola, Florida, and a quite capable one. It was an ebullient Yancey who was introduced to the press interview room, and there he pledged his affection for the Masters and to the goal of winning it, if not in 1967, in some future year. Perhaps it was there that Yancey committed his tactical error, demanding this much of himself before maturing to the ordeal of his most severe opponent, the course.

His Friday round was six strokes higher, but he kept his place. He was still tied with Julius Boros and Bobby Nichols after a 71 on Saturday, but the Sunday round and the tournament went to Gay Brewer. Bert Yancey has never led the Masters again at the end of any day. Sometimes during a round but never after all the players were in. He persisted in his crusade. He flew around the course in a dramatic charge to a 65 on the last round in 1968, but that left him two strokes down to Bob Goalby. He played his most consistent four rounds in 1970, 69-70-72-70, but that left him two strokes behind Bill Casper and Gene Littler, and the fade-out was in effect. He paused now in the locker room to reflect upon his goal after a visit to a bunker had finished him on the 18th hole.

"It takes a lot to win this tournament," he said. "More and more each year, I realize what it takes."

In light of his winnings, one is often inclined to overlook the fact that no contestant has ever finished second more than Ben Hogan — four times — but at the latest count, Tom Weiskopf has tied this record for frustration. However, Weiskopf is still a young man and at the crest of his game. Winning is still within his reach, but to date, 1976, this graduate of Ohio State University which presented Jack Nicklaus to the game, is still among the corps of bridesmaids. The tall, sandy-haired fellow with the wide swath of a swing had gone out in 1969 needing three strokes to catch Bill Casper, who was leading, on Sunday. And did, but was passed by George Archer. Again in 1972, when the leaders were backing up, he needed only a modest 71 to catch Nicklaus, but each used 74 strokes. A gem of consistency in 1974, his 71-69-70-70 gained him only another tie for second.

Then came the glorious gallop through the stretch in 1975 in the hunt with Jack Nicklaus and Johnny Miller. Weiskopf had gone out the leader on Sunday after picking up seven strokes on Nicklaus the day before with a magnificent round of 66. Even to the 69th stroke of the club on Sunday he still had his chance, but an 8- to 10-foot putt passed by the 18th hole on the high side, and he had only another silver medal to add to his trophy case.

"I can't believe I lost this Masters," Weiskopf said, drained and in an emotional morass. "The luck balances out. All I know is that one of these days the putts will drop and I'll win one."

There were others frustrated and repulsed by this very selective chain of golf holes. A review of the rejected could include Ed Dudley, who was Augusta National's first club professional; Sam Byrd, the former New York Yankee outfielder who switched and became quite a successful tournament player; Jim Ferrier, the tall, stoop-shouldered Australian; Jim Jamieson, the affable soul of portliness from Illinois; and the three amateurs who came close in 1947, Frank Stranahan, who later turned professional,

Charlie Coe, tall, somber Oklahoman who chased Gary Player home in 1961, and Billy Joe Patton, the unforgettable, indomitable hillbilly from North Carolina who found himself shoulder to shoulder with the gods in 1954.

Then in 1968 came perhaps the most frustrated entry of them all — Lee Trevino. He had grown up of Mexican-American breeding in Dallas in a two-room dwelling without electricity, water, or central heating and with the earth for a floor. He came to the Masters a developing sensation — brash, loud, short on wardrobe and still trying to learn to live with his new prestige. The austerity and the propriety of Augusta National bewildered him; nevertheless, he played the course for three days as if they were cousins. Teeing off Sunday with Miller Barber, he was only two shots behind the leader, but his score ballooned to an 80 as he chattered and clowned and tried to find a level of peace with the galleries.

It wasn't until 1975 that he finally finished among the leading 24 players. Maturity appeared to be bringing about a softening attitude toward the tournament and the men in the green coats who run it. It was Arnold Palmer who lately said, "This is the kind of tournament that Lee could win, once he sets his mind to it."

The Masters still did not intimidate Trevino to the point that he couldn't have a little spontaneous fun there. Going to the 16th hole one day, he bet a playing companion that he could hit his tee shot across the top of the water and onto the green.

"I took a one-iron, and I hit it flat and made it skip across the water, boop, boop, boopety boop, four times. The water was low and there was no lip on the bank in front of the green. The ball rolled right up on the green, I putted twice and got my par and won my bet," he said.

On the other hand, the Masters has had this intuition to pay off those to whom it feels indebted on occasion — as in the case of Craig Wood in 1941, after twice denying this great, picturesque player; Ralph Guldahl in 1939, after his frustrations of 1937 and 1938; Ben Hogan, who surely had a victory coming after his defeats by Byron Nelson and Herman Keiser; Gay Brewer in 1967, after his loss in the play-off of 1966; Bill Casper in 1970, after his collapse on the front nine in 1969; and Charles Coody in 1971, after taking the lead, then dunking it in the pond at the 15th hole, also in 1969.

As cruel as it sometimes may seem, there is indeed a spirit of compassion rising up out of the soil so graciously blessed and reverently anointed by Robert Tyre Jones, Jr., himself.

Epilogue

Augusta National at rest, a quiet twilight hour after all the players and the galleries have taken leave;
the cupola, the flowered centerpiece in the turnaround, both symbols of the finest golf tournament in the world.

". . . We all drive the other way down Magnolia Lane one more time. . . ."

The grey hours of Sunday afternoon are closing in. The folding chairs still rest on the putting green, vacant now. Presentation rituals have been staged. Bowman Milligan, the keeper of the green coat, with all his plantation courtliness, has made his annual delivery from the clubhouse closet, and the winner has felt the jacket slip around his shoulders. Lights shine softly from the windows of the old clubhouse and the Trophy Room, and inside a few late-stayers are reluctant to let loose of this moment.

From the doorway of the Press Building, a paragon among such facilities in tournament golfing, the hurried chatter of typewriters gushes forth. Men are poised over their machines as if about to spring upon them. Deadlines bear heavily on their racked minds. In Japan, in England, in Canada, in Seattle, in San Antonio, in Boston, and in over 500 points around our globe an office editor waits for their versions of what has happened in another Masters.

Silhouetted in the doorway is the likeness of the champion. Nicklaus. Player. Palmer. Goalby. The year is yours for the picking, but 1953 is your limit in retrospect, for the Press Building was not there before. The victor stands talking happily, willingly, animatedly, openly, sentimentally, draining every sugary drop of ecstasy from his hour. It is precious. The little cone-shaped microphones of tape recorders are thrust in front of his face, but they bother him none now. The words will come out later over the air of some radio station somewhere, and the "man-on-the-scene" for one short remote cue-in will seem to his audience to have had the champion for himself.

Further up the narrow road that runs between the hedges, the parking lot is virtually an open field now. A few cars remain, over here, over there, some in a cluster. The more unhurried are casual in deck chairs, having a last toddy to a good time about to slip their grasp. Meaty fumes arise from a few charcoal cookers, for some are even casual enough to balance the chemistry of their appetites before setting out.

A capricious breeze playfully kicks up little puffs of dust, and they dance around in the growing gloom and are gone. Somehow, it seems a proper signature to the hour, for there are those for whom Augusta suddenly congeals on the banks of the Savannah for one week each spring, then just as abruptly fades away into a nothing state as if it had never been before.

Another Masters has been played. Another champion ordained. Another classic filed away among the notes of American sport, and we all drive the other way down Magnolia Lane one more time, past the sentry at the white brick columns, out onto Washington Road, and each to his own nest.

Top Twenty-Four Finishers

NAME	1st Round	2nd Round	3rd Round	4th Round	Total Score	NAME	1st Round	2nd Round	3rd Round	4th Round	Total Score
1934						**1936**					
Horton Smith	70	72	70	72	284	Horton Smith	74	71	68	72	285
Craig Wood	71	74	69	71	285	Harry Cooper	70	69	71	76	286
Billy Burke	72	71	70	73	286	Gene Sarazen	78	67	72	70	287
Paul Runyan	74	71	70	71	286	Bobby Cruickshank	75	69	74	72	290
Ed Dudley	74	69	71	74	288	Paul Runyan	76	69	70	75	290
Willie MacFarlane	74	73	70	74	291	Ray Mangrum	76	73	68	76	293
Harold McSpaden	77	74	72	69	292	Ed Dudley	75	75	70	73	293
Al Espinosa	75	70	75	72	292	Ky Laffoon	75	70	75	73	293
Jimmy Hines	70	74	74	74	292	John Dawson	77	70	70	77	294
MacDonald Smith	74	70	74	74	292	Henry Picard	75	72	74	73	294
Mortie Dutra	74	75	71	73	293	Denny Shute	76	68	75	77	296
Al Watrous	74	74	71	74	293	Walter Hagen	77	74	73	72	296
Denny Shute	73	73	76	72	294	Byron Nelson	76	71	77	74	298
Robert T. Jones, Jr.	76	74	72	72	294	Wiffy Cox	82	69	75	72	298
Walter Hagen	71	76	70	77	294	Vic Ghezzi	77	70	77	75	299
Ralph Stonehouse	74	70	75	76	295	Jimmy Thomson	76	78	71	74	299
Leo Diegel	73	72	74	76	295	Harold McSpaden	77	75	71	76	299
W. J. Schwartz	75	72	71	78	296	Al Espinosa	72	73	75	79	299
Johnny Revolta	75	72	75	74	296	Orville White	78	73	77	71	299
Ky Laffoon	72	79	72	73	296	Sam Parks, Jr.	76	75	72	77	300
Johnny Golden	71	75	74	77	297	Craig Wood	88	67	69	76	300
Charles Yates	76	72	77	72	297	Tommy Armour	79	74	72	75	300
John Dawson	74	73	76	75	298	Chick Chin	76	74	71	79	300
Henry Picard	71	76	75	76	298	Lawson Little, Jr.	75	75	73	77	300
1935						**1937**					
Gene Sarazen	68	71	73	70	282	Byron Nelson	66	72	75	70	283
Play-off					144	Ralph Guldahl	69	72	68	76	285
Craig Wood	69	72	68	73	282	Ed Dudley	70	71	71	74	286
Play-off					149	Harry Cooper	73	69	71	74	287
Olin Dutra	70	70	70	74	284	Ky Laffoon	73	70	74	73	290
Henry Picard	67	68	76	75	286	Jimmy Thomson	71	73	74	73	291
Denny Shute	73	71	70	73	287	Al Watrous	74	72	71	75	292
Lawson Little, Jr.	74	72	70	72	288	Tommy Armour	73	75	73	72	293
Paul Runyan	70	72	75	72	289	Vic Ghezzi	72	72	72	77	293
Vic Ghezzi	73	71	73	73	290	Jimmy Hines	77	72	68	77	294
Jimmy Hines	70	70	77	74	291	Leonard Dodson	71	75	71	77	294
Byron Nelson	71	74	72	74	291	Wiffy Cox	70	72	77	76	295
Bobby Cruickshank	76	70	73	72	291	Denny Shute	74	75	71	76	296
Joe Turnesa	73	71	74	73	291	Johnny Revolta	71	72	72	81	296
Ray Mangrum	68	71	76	77	292	Clarence Clark	77	75	70	74	296
Johnny Revolta	70	74	73	75	292	Tony Manero	71	72	78	75	296
Sam Parks, Jr.	74	70	74	75	293	Bobby Cruickshank	79	69	71	78	297
Walter Hagen	73	69	72	79	293	Sam Snead	76	72	71	79	298
Al Espinosa	76	72	73	73	294	Horton Smith	75	72	77	75	299
John Dawson	75	72	72	75	294	Lawson Little, Jr.	70	79	74	76	299
Clarence Clark	77	75	73	71	296	Willie MacFarlane	73	76	73	77	299
Charles Yates	75	70	76	75	296	Paul Runyan	74	77	72	76	299
Leo Diegel	72	73	74	77	296	Felix Serafin	75	76	71	77	299
Horton Smith	74	75	74	73	296	Gene Sarazen	74	80	73	73	300
Ed Dudley	73	73	74	76	296						
Harold McSpaden	75	72	75	74	296						

NAME	1st Round	2nd Round	3rd Round	4th Round	Total Score
1938					
Henry Picard	71	72	72	70	285
Ralph Guldahl	73	70	73	71	287
Harry Cooper	68	77	71	71	287
Paul Runyan	71	73	74	70	288
Byron Nelson	73	74	70	73	290
Ed Dudley	70	69	77	75	291
Felix Serafin	72	71	78	70	291
Dick Metz	70	77	74	71	292
Jimmy Thomson	74	70	76	72	292
Jimmy Hines	75	71	75	72	293
Vic Ghezzi	75	74	70	74	293
Lawson Little, Jr.	72	75	74	72	293
Gene Sarazen	78	70	68	79	295
Billy Burke	73	73	76	73	295
Stanley Horne	74	74	77	71	296
Robert T. Jones, Jr.	76	74	72	75	297
Harold McSpaden	72	75	77	73	297
Ray Mangrum	78	72	76	72	298
Bobby Cruickshank	72	75	77	74	298
Tommy Tailer	74	69	75	80	298
Johnny Revolta	73	72	76	77	298
Charles Kocsis	76	73	77	73	299
Horton Smith	75	75	78	71	299
Sam Parks, Jr.	75	75	76	74	300
1939					
Ralph Guldahl	72	68	70	69	279
Sam Snead	70	70	72	68	280
Billy Burke	69	72	71	70	282
Lawson Little, Jr.	72	72	68	70	282
Gene Sarazen	73	66	72	72	283
Craig Wood	72	73	71	68	284
Byron Nelson	71	69	72	75	287
Henry Picard	71	71	76	71	289
Ben Hogan	75	71	72	72	290
Toney Penna	72	75	72	72	291
Ed Dudley	75	75	69	72	291
Vic Ghezzi	73	76	72	72	293
Tommy Armour	71	74	76	72	293
Harold McSpaden	75	72	74	72	293
Denny Shute	78	71	73	72	294
Paul Runyan	73	71	75	76	295
Felix Serafin	74	76	73	72	295
Jimmy Thomson	75	71	73	77	296
Chick Harbert	74	73	75	74	296
Charles Yates	74	73	74	75	296
Tommy Tailer	78	75	73	71	297
Ky Laffoon	72	75	73	78	298
Jimmy Hines	76	73	74	75	298
Frank Moore	75	74	75	74	298

NAME	1st Round	2nd Round	3rd Round	4th Round	Total Score
1940					
Jimmy Demaret	67	72	70	71	280
Lloyd Mangrum	64	75	71	74	284
Byron Nelson	69	72	74	70	285
Ed Dudley	73	72	71	71	287
Harry Cooper	69	75	73	70	287
Willie Goggin	71	72	73	71	287
Henry Picard	71	71	71	75	288
Craig Wood	70	75	67	76	288
Sam Snead	71	72	69	76	288
Toney Penna	73	73	72	72	290
Ben Hogan	73	74	69	74	290
Paul Runyan	72	73	72	74	291
Frank Walsh	73	75	69	74	291
Sam Byrd	73	74	72	73	292
Johnny Farrell	76	72	70	74	292
Ralph Guldahl	74	73	71	74	292
Harold McSpaden	73	71	74	75	293
Charles Yates	72	75	71	75	293
Lawson Little, Jr.	70	77	75	72	294
Ed Oliver, Jr.	73	75	74	72	294
Johnny Bulla	73	73	74	75	295
Dick Metz	71	74	75	75	295
Gene Sarazen	74	71	77	73	295
Al Watrous	75	70	73	77	295
Marvin Ward	74	68	75	78	295
1941					
Craig Wood	66	71	71	72	280
Byron Nelson	71	69	73	70	283
Sam Byrd	73	70	68	74	285
Ben Hogan	71	72	75	68	286
Ed Dudley	73	72	75	68	288
Sam Snead	73	75	72	69	289
Vic Ghezzi	77	71	71	70	289
Lawson Little, Jr.	71	70	74	75	290
Lloyd Mangrum	71	72	72	76	291
Harold McSpaden	75	74	72	70	291
Willie Goggin	71	72	72	76	291
Jimmy Demaret	77	69	71	75	292
Clayton Heafner	73	70	76	73	292
Jimmy Thomson	73	75	72	73	293
Harry Cooper	72	73	75	73	293
Ralph Guldahl	76	71	75	71	293
Jack Ryan	73	74	74	74	295
Denny Shute	77	75	74	70	296
Felix Serafin	72	79	74	72	297
Horton Smith	74	72	77	74	297
Sam Parks, Jr.	75	76	75	71	297
Gene Sarazen	76	72	74	75	297
Toney Penna	73	74	80	70	297
Jimmy Hines	76	74	75	72	297
Richard D. Chapman	76	73	70	78	297
Gene Kunes	76	74	76	71	297
Dick Metz	74	72	75	76	297

NAME	1st Round	2nd Round	3rd Round	4th Round	Total Score
1942					
Byron Nelson	68	67	72	73	280
Play-off					69
Ben Hogan	73	70	67	70	280
Play-off					70
Paul Runyan	67	73	72	71	283
Sam Byrd	68	68	75	74	285
Horton Smith	67	73	74	73	287
Jimmy Demaret	70	70	75	75	290
E. J. Harrison	74	70	71	77	292
Lawson Little, Jr.	71	74	72	75	292
Sam Snead	78	69	72	73	292
Gene Kunes	74	74	74	71	293
Chick Harbert	73	73	72	75	293
Jimmy Thomson	73	70	74	70	294
Chandler Harper	75	75	76	69	295
Willie Goggin	74	70	78	74	296
Bobby Cruickshank	72	79	71	75	297
Jim Ferrier	71	76	80	70	297
Henry Picard	75	72	75	75	297
Harry Cooper	74	77	76	72	299
Harold McSpaden	74	72	79	74	299
Felix Serafin	75	74	77	73	299
Ralph Guldahl	74	74	76	76	300
Toney Penna	74	79	73	75	301
Billy Burke	71	79	80	72	302
Herman Keiser	74	74	78	76	302
Craig Wood	72	75	82	73	302
1946					
Herman Keiser	69	68	71	74	282
Ben Hogan	74	70	69	70	283
Bob Hamilton	75	69	71	72	287
Ky Laffoon	74	73	70	72	289
Jimmy Demaret	75	70	71	73	289
Jim Ferrier	74	72	68	75	289
Sam Snead	74	75	70	71	290
Clayton Heafner	74	69	71	76	290
Byron Nelson	72	73	71	74	290
Chick Harbert	69	75	76	70	290
Jim Foulis	75	70	72	74	291
Cary Middlecoff	72	76	70	74	292
George Schneiter	73	73	72	75	293
Vic Ghezzi	71	79	67	76	293
Fred Haas, Jr.	71	75	68	80	294
Johnny Bulla	72	76	73	74	295
Lloyd Mangrum	76	75	72	72	295
Claude Harmon	76	75	74	71	296
Chandler Harper	74	76	73	74	297
Frank Stranahan	76	74	73	75	298
Felix Serafin	76	75	79	69	299
Lawson Little, Jr.	74	74	78	73	299
Toney Penna	71	73	80	75	299
Horton Smith	78	77	75	69	299

NAME	1st Round	2nd Round	3rd Round	4th Round	Total Score
1947					
Jimmy Demaret	69	71	70	71	281
Byron Nelson	69	72	72	70	283
Frank Stranahan	73	72	70	68	283
Ben Hogan	75	68	71	70	284
Harold McSpaden	74	69	70	71	284
Henry Picard	73	70	72	71	286
Jim Ferrier	70	71	73	72	286
Ed Oliver, Jr.	70	72	74	71	287
Chandler Harper	77	72	68	70	287
Lloyd Mangrum	76	73	68	70	287
Toney Penna	71	70	75	71	287
Dick Metz	72	72	72	71	287
Johnny Bulla	70	75	74	69	288
Lawson Little, Jr.	71	71	76	71	289
Bobby Locke	74	74	71	70	289
Richard D. Chapman	72	71	74	72	289
Johnny Palmer	70	73	74	73	290
Herman Barron	71	71	74	74	290
Fred Haas, Jr.	70	74	73	73	290
Denny Shute	73	75	72	71	291
Vic Ghezzi	73	77	71	71	292
Horton Smith	72	70	76	75	293
Sam Snead	72	71	75	75	293
Herman Keiser	74	75	73	72	294
Ellsworth Vines	75	71	75	73	294
1948					
Claude Harmon	70	70	69	70	279
Cary Middlecoff	74	71	69	70	284
Chick Harbert	71	70	70	76	287
Jim Ferrier	71	71	75	71	288
Lloyd Mangrum	69	73	75	71	288
Ed Furgol	70	72	73	74	289
Ben Hogan	70	71	77	71	289
Byron Nelson	71	73	72	74	290
Harry Todd	72	67	80	71	290
Herman Keiser	70	72	76	73	291
Bobby Locke	71	71	74	75	291
Dick Metz	71	72	75	73	291
Johnny Bulla	74	72	76	71	293
E. J. Harrison	73	77	73	70	293
Skee Riegel	71	74	73	75	293
Al Smith	73	73	74	74	294
Sam Snead	74	75	72	73	294
Jimmy Demaret	73	72	78	72	295
Ed Dudley	73	76	75	71	295
Vic Ghezzi	75	73	73	74	295
Bob Hamilton	72	72	76	75	295
Fred Haas, Jr.	75	75	76	69	295
Art Bell	71	74	74	77	296
Gene Sarazen	77	74	73	72	296

NAME	1st Round	2nd Round	3rd Round	4th Round	Total Score
1949					
Sam Snead	73	75	67	67	282
Johnny Bulla	74	73	69	69	285
Lloyd Mangrum	69	74	72	70	285
Johnny Palmer	73	71	70	72	286
Jim Turnesa	73	72	71	70	286
Lew Worsham, Jr.	76	75	70	68	289
Joe Kirkwood, Jr.	73	72	70	75	290
Jimmy Demaret	76	72	73	71	292
Clayton Heafner	71	74	72	75	292
Byron Nelson	75	70	74	73	292
Claude Harmon	73	75	73	72	293
Herman Keiser	75	68	78	72	293
Herman Barron	73	75	71	75	294
Leland Gibson	71	77	74	72	294
Bobby Locke	74	74	74	72	294
Charles R. Coe	77	72	72	74	295
John W. Dawson	78	72	72	73	295
Jim Ferrier	77	72	67	79	295
Tony Holguin	81	70	71	74	296
Frank Stranahan	70	77	75	74	296
Pete Cooper	76	75	72	74	297
Henry Picard	74	77	73	73	297
Bob Hamilton	77	79	69	73	298
E. J. Harrison	73	78	75	72	298
Lawson Little, Jr.	72	77	73	76	298
Cary Middlecoff	76	77	72	73	298
Toney Penna	74	76	76	72	298
Horton Smith	75	72	78	73	298
1950					
Jimmy Demaret	70	72	72	69	283
Jim Ferrier	70	67	73	75	285
Sam Snead	71	74	70	72	287
Ben Hogan	73	68	71	76	288
Byron Nelson	75	70	69	74	288
Lloyd Mangrum	76	74	73	68	291
Clayton Heafner	74	77	69	72	292
Cary Middlecoff	75	76	68	73	292
Lawson Little, Jr.	70	73	75	75	293
Fred Haas, Jr.	74	76	73	71	294
Gene Sarazen	80	70	72	72	294
Roberto de Vicenzo	76	76	73	71	296
Horton Smith	70	79	75	72	296
Skip Alexander	78	74	73	72	297
Vic Ghezzi	78	75	70	74	297
Leland Gibson	78	73	72	74	297
Herman Keiser	75	72	75	75	297
Joe Kirkwood, Jr.	75	74	77	71	297
Henry Picard	74	71	77	75	297
Frank Stranahan	74	79	73	71	297
George Fazio	73	74	78	73	298
Toney Penna	71	75	77	75	298
Skee Riegel	69	75	78	76	298
Chick Harbert	76	75	73	75	299
Johnny Palmer	72	76	76	75	299

NAME	1st Round	2nd Round	3rd Round	4th Round	Total Score
1951					
Ben Hogan	70	72	70	68	280
Skee Riegel	73	68	70	71	282
Lloyd Mangrum	69	74	70	73	286
Lew Worsham, Jr.	71	71	72	72	286
Dave Douglas	74	69	72	73	288
Lawson Little, Jr.	72	73	72	72	289
Jim Ferrier	74	70	74	72	290
Johnny Bulla	71	72	73	75	291
Byron Nelson	71	73	73	74	291
Sam Snead	69	74	68	80	291
Jack Burke, Jr.	73	72	74	73	292
Charles R. Coe	76	71	73	73	293
Cary Middlecoff	73	73	69	78	293
Gene Sarazen	75	74	73	71	293
Ed Furgol	80	71	72	71	294
E. J. Harrison	76	71	76	71	294
Julius Boros	76	72	74	73	295
George Fazio	68	74	74	80	296
Bob Toski	75	73	73	75	296
Al Besselink	76	73	71	77	297
Richard D. Chapman	72	76	72	77	297
Clayton Heafner	74	72	73	78	297
Joe Kirkwood, Jr.	73	71	78	75	297
Roberto de Vicenzo	75	74	74	74	297
1952					
Sam Snead	70	67	77	72	286
Jack Burke, Jr.	76	67	78	69	290
Al Besselink	70	76	71	74	291
Tommy Bolt	71	71	75	74	291
Jim Ferrier	72	70	77	72	291
Lloyd Mangrum	71	74	75	72	292
Julius Boros	73	73	76	71	293
Fred Hawkins	71	73	78	71	293
Ben Hogan	70	70	74	79	293
Lew Worsham, Jr.	71	75	73	74	293
Cary Middlecoff	72	72	72	78	294
Johnny Palmer	69	74	75	77	295
Johnny Revolta	71	71	77	77	296
George Fazio	72	71	78	76	297
Claude Harmon	73	74	77	73	297
Charles Kocsis	75	78	71	73	297
Ted Kroll	74	74	76	73	297
Skee Riegel	75	71	78	73	297
Joe Kirkwood, Jr.	71	77	74	76	298
Frank Stranahan	72	74	76	76	298
Doug Ford	71	74	79	75	299
Bobby Locke	74	71	79	75	299
E. Harvie Ward, Jr.	72	71	78	78	299
Arnold Blum	74	77	77	74	302
Clayton Heafner	76	74	74	78	302
Byron Nelson	72	75	78	77	302

NAME	1st Round	2nd Round	3rd Round	4th Round	Total Score

1953

NAME	1st Round	2nd Round	3rd Round	4th Round	Total Score
Ben Hogan	70	69	66	69	274
Ed Oliver, Jr.	69	73	67	70	279
Lloyd Mangrum	74	68	71	69	282
Bob Hamilton	71	69	70	73	283
Tommy Bolt	71	75	68	71	285
Chick Harbert	68	73	70	74	285
Ted Kroll	71	70	73	72	286
Jack Burke, Jr.	78	69	69	71	287
Al Besselink	69	75	70	74	288
Julius Boros	73	71	75	70	289
Chandler Harper	74	72	69	74	289
Fred Hawkins	75	70	74	70	289
Johnny Palmer	74	73	72	71	290
Frank Stranahan	72	75	69	75	291
E. Harvie Ward, Jr.	73	74	69	75	291
Charles R. Coe	75	74	72	71	292
Dick Mayer	73	72	71	76	292
Sam Snead	71	75	71	75	292
Jim Ferrier	74	71	76	71	292
Earl Stewart, Jr.	75	72	70	75	292
Jerry Barber	73	76	72	72	293
Doug Ford	73	73	72	75	293
Leland Gibson	73	71	72	78	294
Al Mengert	77	70	75	72	294
Dick Metz	73	72	71	78	294

1954

NAME	1st Round	2nd Round	3rd Round	4th Round	Total Score
Sam Snead	74	73	70	72	289
Play-off					70
Ben Hogan	72	73	69	75	289
Play-off					71
Billy Joe Patton	70	74	75	71	290
E. J. Harrison	70	79	74	68	291
Lloyd Mangrum	71	75	76	69	291
Jerry Barber	74	76	71	71	292
Jack Burke, Jr.	71	77	73	71	292
Bob Rosburg	73	73	76	70	292
Al Besselink	74	74	74	72	294
Cary Middlecoff	73	76	70	75	294
Richard D. Chapman	75	75	75	70	295
Tommy Bolt	73	74	72	77	296
Chick Harbert	73	75	75	73	296
Byron Nelson	73	76	74	73	296
Lew Worsham, Jr.	74	74	74	74	296
Julius Boros	76	79	68	74	297
Jay Hebert	79	74	74	70	297
Peter Thomson	76	72	76	73	297
Ken Venturi	76	74	73	74	297
Charles R. Coe	76	75	73	74	298
E. Harvie Ward, Jr.	78	75	74	71	298
Walter Burkemo	74	77	75	73	299
Pete Cooper	73	76	75	75	299
Marty Furgol	76	79	75	69	299
Gene Littler	79	75	73	72	299
Ed Oliver, Jr.	75	75	75	74	299
Earl Stewart, Jr.	78	75	75	71	299
Bob Toski	80	74	71	74	299

1955

NAME	1st Round	2nd Round	3rd Round	4th Round	Total Score
Cary Middlecoff	72	65	72	70	279
Ben Hogan	73	68	72	73	286
Sam Snead	72	71	74	70	287
Bob Rosburg	72	72	72	73	289
Mike Souchak	71	74	72	72	289
Julius Boros	71	75	72	71	289
Lloyd Mangrum	74	73	72	72	291
E. Harvie Ward, Jr.	77	69	75	71	292
Stan Leonard	77	73	68	74	292
Dick Mayer	78	72	72	71	293
Byron Nelson	72	75	74	72	293
Arnold Palmer	76	76	72	69	293
Skee Riegel	73	73	73	75	294
Jack Burke, Jr.	67	76	71	80	294
Jay Hebert	75	74	74	72	295
Walter Burkemo	73	73	72	77	295
Frank Stranahan	77	76	71	71	295
Joe Conrad	77	71	74	75	297
Peter Thomson	74	73	74	76	297
Johnny Palmer	77	73	72	75	297
Billy Maxwell	77	72	77	71	297
Gene Littler	75	72	76	75	298
Tommy Bolt	76	70	77	75	298
Hillman Robbins, Jr.	77	76	74	72	299
Ed Furgol	74	72	78	75	299
Pete Cooper	73	73	78	75	299

1956

NAME	1st Round	2nd Round	3rd Round	4th Round	Total Score
Jack Burke, Jr.	72	71	75	71	289
Ken Venturi	66	69	75	80	290
Cary Middlecoff	67	72	75	77	291
Lloyd Mangrum	72	74	72	74	292
Sam Snead	73	76	72	71	292
Jerry Barber	71	72	76	75	294
Doug Ford	70	72	75	77	294
Shelley Mayfield	68	74	80	74	296
Tommy Bolt	68	74	78	76	296
Ben Hogan	69	78	74	75	296
Johnny Palmer	76	74	74	73	297
Pete Cooper	72	70	77	79	298
Gene Littler	73	77	74	74	298
Billy Joe Patton	70	76	79	73	298
Sam Urzetta	73	75	76	74	298
Bob Rosburg	70	74	81	74	299
Walter Burkemo	72	74	78	76	300
Hillman Robbins, Jr.	73	73	78	76	300
Mike Souchak	73	73	74	80	300
Roberto de Vicenzo	75	72	78	75	300
Arnold Palmer	73	75	74	79	301
Frank Stranahan	72	75	79	76	302
Jim Turnesa	74	74	74	80	302
Julius Boros	73	78	72	80	303
Dow Finsterwald	74	73	79	77	303
Ed Furgol	74	75	78	76	303
Stan Leonard	75	75	79	74	303
Al Mengert	74	72	79	78	303

NAME	1st Round	2nd Round	3rd Round	4th Round	Total Score

1957

NAME	1st Round	2nd Round	3rd Round	4th Round	Total Score
Doug Ford	72	73	72	66	283
Sam Snead	72	68	74	72	286
Jimmy Demaret	72	70	75	70	287
E. Harvie Ward, Jr.	73	71	71	73	288
Peter Thomson	72	73	73	71	289
Ed Furgol	73	71	72	74	290
Jack Burke, Jr.	71	72	74	74	291
Dow Finsterwald	74	74	73	70	291
Arnold Palmer	73	73	69	76	291
Jay Hebert	74	72	76	70	292
Marty Furgol	73	74	73	73	293
Stan Leonard	75	72	68	78	293
Frank M. Taylor, Jr.	74	74	77	69	294
Henry Cotton	73	73	72	76	294
Ken Venturi	74	76	74	70	294
Al Balding	73	73	73	76	295
Billy Casper, Jr.	75	75	75	70	295
Mike Fetchick	74	73	72	76	295
Fred Hawkins	75	74	72	74	295
Byron Nelson	74	72	73	76	295
Bruce Crampton	72	75	78	71	296
Al Mengert	75	75	71	75	296
Henry Ransom	75	73	72	76	296
Johnny Palmer	77	73	73	74	297
Gary Player	77	72	75	73	297

1958

NAME	1st Round	2nd Round	3rd Round	4th Round	Total Score
Arnold Palmer	70	73	68	73	284
Doug Ford	74	71	70	70	285
Fred Hawkins	71	75	68	71	285
Stan Leonard	72	70	73	71	286
Ken Venturi	68	72	74	72	286
Cary Middlecoff	70	73	69	75	287
Art Wall, Jr.	71	72	70	74	287
Billy Joe Patton	72	69	73	74	288
Claude Harmon	71	76	72	70	289
Jay Hebert	72	73	73	71	289
Billy Maxwell	71	70	72	76	289
Al Mengert	73	71	69	76	289
Sam Snead	72	71	68	79	290
Jimmy Demaret	69	79	70	73	291
Ben Hogan	72	77	69	73	291
Mike Souchak	72	75	73	71	291
Dow Finsterwald	72	71	74	75	292
Chick Harbert	69	74	73	76	292
Bo Wininger	69	73	71	79	292
Billy Casper, Jr.	76	71	72	74	293
Byron Nelson	71	77	74	71	293
Phil Rodgers	77	72	73	72	294
Charles R. Coe	73	76	69	77	295
Ted Kroll	73	75	75	72	295
Peter Thomson	72	74	73	76	295

1959

NAME	1st Round	2nd Round	3rd Round	4th Round	Total Score
Art Wall, Jr.	73	74	71	66	284
Cary Middlecoff	74	71	68	72	285
Arnold Palmer	71	70	71	74	286
Dick Mayer	73	75	71	68	287
Stan Leonard	69	74	69	75	287
Charles R. Coe	74	74	67	73	288
Fred Hawkins	77	71	68	73	289
Julius Boros	75	69	74	72	290
Jay Hebert	72	73	72	73	290
Gene Littler	72	75	72	71	290
Billy Maxwell	73	71	72	74	290
Billy Joe Patton	75	70	71	74	290
Gary Player	73	75	71	71	290
Chick Harbert	74	72	74	71	291
Chandler Harper	71	74	74	72	291
Ted Kroll	76	71	73	71	291
Ed Oliver, Jr.	75	69	73	74	291
Dow Finsterwald	79	68	73	72	292
Jack Fleck	74	71	71	76	292
William Hyndman III	73	72	76	71	292
Bo Wininger	75	70	72	75	292
Walter Burkemo	75	70	71	77	293
Charles Kocsis	73	75	70	75	293
Sam Snead	74	73	72	74	293

1960

NAME	1st Round	2nd Round	3rd Round	4th Round	Total Score
Arnold Palmer	67	73	72	70	282
Ken Venturi	73	69	71	70	283
Dow Finsterwald	71	70	72	71	284
Billy Casper, Jr.	71	71	71	74	287
Julius Boros	72	71	70	75	288
Walter Burkemo	72	69	75	73	289
Ben Hogan	73	68	72	76	289
Gary Player	72	71	72	74	289
Lionel Hebert	74	70	73	73	290
Stan Leonard	72	72	72	74	290
Jack Burke, Jr.	72	72	74	74	292
Sam Snead	73	74	72	73	292
Ted Kroll	72	76	71	74	293
Jack Nicklaus	75	71	72	75	293
Billy Joe Patton	75	72	74	72	293
Bruce Crampton	74	73	75	72	294
Claude Harmon	69	72	75	78	294
Fred Hawkins	69	78	72	75	294
Mike Souchak	72	75	72	75	294
Tommy Bolt	73	74	75	73	295
Don January	70	72	74	79	295
Ed Oliver, Jr.	74	75	73	73	295
Bob Rosburg	74	74	71	76	295
Frank M. Taylor, Jr.	70	74	73	78	295

NAME	1st Round	2nd Round	3rd Round	4th Round	Total Score

1961

NAME	1st Round	2nd Round	3rd Round	4th Round	Total Score
Gary Player	69	68	69	74	280
Charles R. Coe	72	71	69	69	281
Arnold Palmer	68	69	73	71	281
Tommy Bolt	72	71	74	68	285
Don January	74	68	72	71	285
Paul Harney	71	73	68	74	286
Jack Burke, Jr.	76	70	68	73	287
Billy Casper, Jr.	72	77	69	69	287
Bill Collins	74	72	67	74	287
Jack Nicklaus	70	75	70	72	287
Walter Burkemo	74	69	73	72	288
Robert Gardner	74	71	72	71	288
Doug Sanders	76	71	68	73	288
Ken Venturi	72	71	72	73	288
Stan Leonard	72	74	71	72	289
Gene Littler	72	73	72	72	289
Bob Rosburg	68	73	73	75	289
Sam Snead	74	73	69	73	289
Dick Mayer	76	72	70	73	291
Johnny Pott	71	75	72	73	291
Peter Thomson	73	76	68	74	291
Roberto de Vicenzo	73	74	71	74	292
Lew Worsham	74	71	73	74	292
Antonio Cerda	73	73	72	75	293
Fred Hawkins	74	75	72	72	293
Ted Kroll	73	70	72	78	293

1962

NAME	1st Round	2nd Round	3rd Round	4th Round	Total Score
Arnold Palmer	70	66	69	75	280
Play-off					68
Gary Player	67	71	71	71	280
Play-off					71
Dow Finsterwald	74	68	65	73	280
Play-off					77
Gene Littler	71	68	71	72	282
Mike Souchak	70	72	74	71	287
Jimmy Demaret	73	73	71	70	287
Jerry Barber	72	72	69	74	287
Billy Maxwell	71	73	72	71	287
Ken Venturi	75	70	71	72	288
Charles R. Coe	72	74	71	71	288
Jack Fleck	72	75	74	69	290
Julius Boros	69	73	72	76	290
Gay Brewer, Jr.	74	71	70	75	290
Harold Henning	75	73	72	70	290
Billy Casper, Jr.	73	73	73	72	291
Paul Harney	74	71	74	72	291
Jack Nicklaus	74	75	70	72	291
Gardner E. Dickinson, Jr.	70	71	72	78	291
Sam Snead	72	75	70	74	291
Jacky Cupit	73	73	72	74	292
Don January	71	73	74	74	292
Johnny Pott	77	71	75	69	292
Lionel Hebert	72	73	71	76	292
Al Balding	75	68	78	72	293

1963

NAME	1st Round	2nd Round	3rd Round	4th Round	Total Score
Jack Nicklaus	74	66	74	72	286
Tony Lema	74	69	74	70	287
Julius Boros	76	69	71	72	288
Sam Snead	70	73	74	71	288
Dow Finsterwald	74	73	73	69	289
Ed Furgol	70	71	74	74	289
Gary Player	71	74	74	70	289
Bo Wininger	69	72	77	72	290
Don January	73	75	72	71	291
Arnold Palmer	74	73	73	71	291
Billy Casper, Jr.	79	72	71	70	292
Bruce Crampton	74	74	72	72	292
Doug Ford	75	73	75	69	292
Mike Souchak	69	70	79	74	292
Robert J. Charles	74	72	76	71	293
Chen Ching-po	76	71	71	75	293
Billy Maxwell	72	75	76	70	293
Dick Mayer	73	70	80	70	293
Mason Rudolph	75	72	72	74	293
Dan Sikes	74	76	72	71	293
Stan Leonard	74	72	73	75	294
Johnny Pott	75	76	74	69	294
Art Wall, Jr.	75	74	73	72	294
Wes Ellis, Jr.	74	72	79	70	295
Gene Littler	77	72	78	68	295
Bobby Nichols	76	74	73	72	295

1964

NAME	1st Round	2nd Round	3rd Round	4th Round	Total Score
Arnold Palmer	69	68	69	70	276
Dave Marr	70	73	69	70	282
Jack Nicklaus	71	73	71	67	282
Bruce Devlin	72	72	67	73	284
Billy Casper, Jr.	76	72	69	69	286
Jim Ferrier	71	73	69	73	286
Paul Harney	73	72	71	70	286
Gary Player	69	72	72	73	286
Dow Finsterwald	71	72	75	69	287
Ben Hogan	73	75	67	72	287
Tony Lema	75	68	74	70	287
Mike Souchak	73	74	70	70	287
Peter J. Butler	72	72	69	75	288
Al Geiberger	75	73	70	70	288
Gene Littler	70	72	78	68	288
Johnny Pott	74	70	71	73	288
Dan Sikes	76	68	71	73	288
Don January	70	72	75	72	289
Billy Maxwell	73	73	69	74	289
Mason Rudolph	75	72	69	73	289
Bruce Crampton	74	72	73	71	290
Kel Nagle	69	77	71	73	290
Juan Rodriguez	71	73	73	73	290
Bo Wininger	74	71	69	76	290

NAME	1st Round	2nd Round	3rd Round	4th Round	Total Score
1965					
Jack Nicklaus	67	71	64	69	271
Arnold Palmer	70	68	72	70	280
Gary Player	65	73	69	73	280
Mason Rudolph	70	75	66	72	283
Dan Sikes	67	72	71	75	285
Gene Littler	71	74	67	74	286
Ramon Sota	71	73	70	72	286
Frank Beard	68	77	72	70	287
Tommy Bolt	69	78	69	71	287
George Knudson	72	73	69	74	288
Tommy Aaron	67	74	71	77	289
Bruce Crampton	72	72	74	71	289
Paul Harney	74	74	71	70	289
Doug Sanders	69	72	74	74	289
George Bayer	69	74	75	72	290
Bruce Devlin	71	76	73	70	290
Wes Ellis, Jr.	69	76	72	73	290
Tommy Jacobs	71	74	72	73	290
Kel Nagle	75	70	74	71	290
Byron Nelson	70	74	72	74	290
Dow Finsterwald	72	75	72	72	291
Ben Hogan	71	75	71	74	291
Tony Lema	67	73	77	74	291
Terry Dill	72	73	75	72	292
Al Geiberger	75	72	74	71	292
1966					
Jack Nicklaus	68	76	72	72	288
Play-off					70
Tommy Jacobs	75	71	70	72	288
Play-off					72
Gay Brewer, Jr.	74	72	72	70	288
Play-off					78
Arnold Palmer	74	70	74	72	290
Doug Sanders	74	70	75	71	290
Don January	71	73	73	75	292
George Knudson	73	76	72	71	292
Raymond L. Floyd	72	73	74	74	293
Paul Harney	75	68	76	74	293
Billy Casper, Jr.	71	75	76	72	294
Jay Hebert	72	74	73	75	294
Bob Rosburg	73	71	76	74	294
Tommy Aaron	74	73	77	71	295
Peter J. Butler	72	71	79	73	295
Ben Hogan	74	71	73	77	295
Ken Venturi	75	74	73	74	296
Tommy Bolt	75	72	78	72	297
Bruce Crampton	74	75	71	77	297
Terry Dill	75	72	74	76	297
Doug Ford	75	73	73	76	297
Phil Rodgers	76	73	75	73	297
Frank Beard	77	71	77	73	298
Chen Ching-po	75	77	76	70	298
Roberto de Vicenzo	74	76	74	74	298
Harold R. Henning	77	74	70	77	298
Tony Lema	74	74	74	76	298
Bobby Nichols	77	73	74	74	298

NAME	1st Round	2nd Round	3rd Round	4th Round	Total Score
1967					
Gay Brewer, Jr.	73	68	72	67	280
Bobby Nichols	72	69	70	70	281
Bert Yancey	67	73	71	73	284
Arnold Palmer	73	73	70	69	285
Julius Boros	71	70	70	75	286
Paul Harney	73	71	74	69	287
Gary Player	75	69	72	71	287
Tommy Aaron	75	68	74	71	288
Lionel Hebert	77	71	67	73	288
Roberto de Vicenzo	73	72	74	71	290
Bruce Devlin	74	70	75	71	290
Ben Hogan	74	73	66	77	290
Mason Rudolph	72	76	72	70	290
Sam Snead	72	76	71	71	290
Jacky Cupit	73	76	67	75	291
George Archer	75	67	72	78	292
Wes Ellis, Jr.	79	71	74	68	292
Tony Jacklin	71	70	74	77	292
Dave Marr	73	74	70	75	292
Doug Sanders	74	72	73	73	292
Jay Hebert	72	77	68	76	293
Bob Rosburg	73	72	76	72	293
Ken Venturi	76	73	71	73	293
Peter J. Butler	72	73	77	72	294
Billy Casper, Jr.	70	74	75	75	294
1968					
Bob Goalby	70	70	71	66	277
Roberto de Vicenzo	69	73	70	66	278
Bert Yancey	71	71	72	65	279
Bruce Devlin	69	73	69	69	280
Frank Beard	75	65	71	70	281
Jack Nicklaus	69	71	74	67	281
Tommy Aaron	69	72	72	69	282
Ray Floyd	71	71	69	71	282
Lionel Hebert	72	71	71	68	282
Jerry Pittman	70	73	70	69	282
Gary Player	72	67	71	72	282
Miller Barber	75	69	68	71	283
Doug Sanders	76	69	70	68	283
Don January	71	68	72	73	284
Mason Rudolph	73	73	72	66	284
Julius Boros	73	71	70	71	285
Billy Casper, Jr.	68	75	73	69	285
Tom Weiskopf	74	71	69	71	285
Bob Charles	75	71	70	70	286
Dave Marr	74	71	71	71	287
Kermit Zarley	70	73	74	70	287
George Archer	75	71	72	70	288
Gardner Dickinson, Jr.	74	71	72	71	288
Marvin Giles III	71	72	72	73	288
Harold R. Henning	72	71	71	74	288
Tony Jacklin	69	73	74	72	288
Art Wall, Jr.	74	74	73	67	288

NAME	1st Round	2nd Round	3rd Round	4th Round	Total Score
1969					
George Archer	67	73	69	72	281
Billy Casper, Jr.	66	71	71	74	282
George Knudson	70	73	69	70	282
Tom Weiskopf	71	71	69	71	282
Charles Coody	74	68	69	72	283
Don January	74	73	70	66	283
Miller Barber	71	71	68	74	284
Tommy Aaron	71	71	73	70	285
Lionel Hebert	69	73	70	73	285
Gene Littler	69	75	70	71	285
Mason Rudolph	69	73	74	70	286
Dan Sikes	69	71	73	74	287
Bruce Crampton	69	73	74	72	288
Al Geiberger	71	71	74	72	288
Harold R. Henning	73	72	71	72	288
Takaaki Kono	71	75	68	74	288
Bert Yancey	69	75	71	73	288
Dave Stockton	71	71	75	72	289
Frank Beard	72	74	70	74	290
Deane Beman	74	73	74	69	290
Bruce Devlin	67	70	76	77	290
Dale Douglass	73	72	71	74	290
Lee Trevino	72	74	75	69	290
Jack Burke, Jr.	73	72	70	76	291
Dave Hill	75	73	72	71	291
Jack Nicklaus	68	75	72	76	291
1970					
Billy Casper, Jr.	72	68	68	71	279
Play-off					69
Gene Littler	69	70	70	70	279
Play-off					74
Gary Player	74	68	68	70	280
Bert Yancey	69	70	72	70	281
Tommy Aaron	68	74	69	72	283
Dave Hill	73	70	70	70	283
Dave Stockton	72	72	69	70	283
Jack Nicklaus	71	75	69	69	284
Frank Beard	71	76	68	70	285
Bob Lunn	70	70	75	72	287
Juan Rodriguez	70	76	73	68	287
Charles Coody	70	74	67	77	288
Bert Greene	75	71	70	72	288
Tony Jacklin	73	74	70	71	288
Don January	76	73	69	70	288
Takaaki Kono	75	68	71	74	288
Bob Charles	75	71	71	72	289
Howie Johnson	75	71	73	71	290
Dick Lotz	74	72	72	72	290
Orville Moody	73	72	71	74	290
Miller Barber	76	73	77	65	291
Terry Wilcox	79	70	70	72	291
Deane Beman	74	72	72	74	292
Charles R. Coe	74	71	72	75	292
Julius Boros	75	71	74	72	292
Bob Murphy	78	70	73	71	292
Sam Snead	76	73	71	72	292
Tom Weiskopf	73	73	72	74	292

NAME	1st Round	2nd Round	3rd Round	4th Round	Total Score
1971					
Charles Coody	66	73	70	70	279
John Miller	72	73	68	68	281
Jack Nicklaus	70	71	68	72	281
Don January	69	69	73	72	283
Gene Littler	72	69	73	69	283
Gary Player	72	72	71	69	284
Ken Still	72	71	72	69	284
Tom Weiskopf	71	69	72	72	284
Frank Beard	74	73	69	70	286
Roberto de Vicenzo	76	69	72	69	286
Dave Stockton	72	73	69	72	286
Bert Greene	73	73	71	70	287
Billy Casper, Jr.	72	73	71	72	288
Bruce Devlin	72	70	72	74	288
Ray Floyd	69	75	73	71	288
Hale Irwin	69	72	71	76	288
Bob Murphy	69	70	76	73	288
Bruce Crampton	73	72	74	70	289
Arnold Palmer	73	72	71	73	289
Dave Eichelberger	76	71	70	73	290
Orville Moody	79	69	70	72	290
Tommy Aaron	76	72	74	69	291
Bobby Mitchell	72	70	74	75	291
Al Geiberger	73	75	72	72	292
Dick Lotz	77	72	73	70	292
Steven Melnyk	73	70	75	74	292
1972					
Jack Nicklaus	68	71	73	74	286
Bruce Crampton	72	75	69	73	289
Bobby Mitchell	73	72	71	73	289
Tom Weiskopf	74	71	70	74	289
Homero Blancas	76	71	69	74	290
Bruce Devlin	74	75	70	71	290
Jerry Heard	73	71	72	74	290
Jim Jamieson	72	70	71	77	290
Jerry McGee	73	74	71	72	290
Gary Player	73	75	72	71	291
Dave Stockton	76	70	74	71	291
George Archer	73	75	72	72	292
Charles Coody	73	70	74	75	292
Al Geiberger	76	70	74	72	292
Steve Melnyk	72	72	74	74	292
Bert Yancey	72	69	76	75	292
Billy Casper, Jr.	75	71	74	74	294
Bob Goalby	73	76	72	73	294
Ben Crenshaw	73	74	74	74	295
Takaaki Kono	76	72	73	74	295
Lanny Wadkins	72	72	77	74	295
Bob Charles	72	76	74	74	296
Roberto de Vicenzo	75	69	76	76	296
Gardner Dickinson	77	72	73	74	296
Hubert Green	75	74	74	73	296
Paul Harney	71	69	75	81	296

NAME	1st Round	2nd Round	3rd Round	4th Round	Total Score
1973					
Tommy Aaron	68	73	74	68	283
J. C. Snead	70	71	73	70	284
Jim Jamieson	73	71	70	71	285
Jack Nicklaus	69	77	73	66	285
Peter Oosterhuis	73	70	68	74	285
Bob Goalby	73	70	71	74	288
Johnny Miller	75	69	71	73	288
Bruce Devlin	73	72	72	72	289
Masashi Ozaki	69	74	73	73	289
Gay Brewer, Jr.	75	66	74	76	291
Gardner Dickinson	74	70	72	75	291
Don January	75	71	75	70	291
Chi Chi Rodriguez	72	70	73	76	291
Hubert Green	72	74	75	71	292
Mason Rudolph	72	72	77	71	292
Dave Stockton	72	74	71	75	292
Billy Casper	75	73	72	73	293
Bob Dickson	70	71	76	76	293
Lou Graham	77	73	72	71	293
Babe Hiskey	74	73	72	74	293
Gene Littler	77	72	71	73	293
Kermit Zarley	74	71	77	71	293
Phil Rodgers	71	75	75	73	294
Frank Beard	73	75	71	76	295
Ben Crenshaw	73	72	74	76	295
Paul Harney	77	71	74	73	295
Bobby Nichols	79	72	76	68	295
Arnold Palmer	77	72	76	70	295
1974					
Gary Player	71	71	66	70	278
Dave Stockton	71	66	70	73	280
Tom Weiskopf	71	69	70	70	280
Jim Colbert	67	72	69	73	281
Hale Irwin	68	70	72	71	281
Jack Nicklaus	69	71	72	69	281
Bobby Nichols	73	68	68	73	282
Phil Rodgers	72	69	68	73	282
Maurice Bembridge	73	74	72	64	283
Hubert Green	68	70	74	71	283
Bruce Crampton	73	72	69	70	284
Jerry Heard	70	70	73	71	284
Dave Hill	71	72	70	71	284
Arnold Palmer	76	71	70	67	284
Bud Allin	73	73	70	69	285
Miller Barber	75	67	72	71	285
Ralph Johnston	72	71	70	72	285
Johnny Miller	72	74	69	70	285
Dan Sikes	69	71	74	71	285
Chi Chi Rodriguez	70	74	71	71	286
Sam Snead	72	72	71	71	286
Frank Beard	69	70	72	76	287
Ben Crenshaw	75	70	70	72	287
Ray Floyd	69	72	76	70	287
Bob Goalby	76	71	72	68	287

NAME	1st Round	2nd Round	3rd Round	4th Round	Total Score
1975					
Jack Nicklaus	68	67	73	68	276
Johnny Miller	75	71	65	66	277
Tom Weiskopf	69	72	66	70	277
Hale Irwin	73	74	71	64	282
Bobby Nichols	67	74	72	69	282
Billy Casper	70	70	73	70	283
Dave Hill	75	71	70	68	284
Hubert Green	74	71	70	70	285
Tom Watson	70	70	72	73	285
Tom Kite	72	74	71	69	286
J. C. Snead	69	72	75	70	286
Lee Trevino	71	70	74	71	286
Arnold Palmer	69	71	75	72	287
Larry Ziegler	71	73	74	69	287
Bobby Cole	73	71	73	71	288
Rod Curl	72	70	76	70	288
Bruce Devlin	72	70	76	70	288
Allen Miller	68	75	72	73	288
Art Wall, Jr.	72	74	72	70	288
Bud Allin	73	69	73	74	289
Ralph Johnston	74	73	69	73	289
Hugh Baiocchi	76	72	72	70	290
Pat Fitzsimons	73	68	79	70	290
Gene Littler	72	72	72	74	290
Graham Marsh	75	70	74	71	290
1976					
Ray Floyd	65	66	70	70	271
Ben Crenshaw	70	70	72	67	279
Jack Nicklaus	67	69	73	73	282
Larry Ziegler	67	71	72	72	282
Charles Coody	72	69	70	74	285
Hale Irwin	71	77	67	70	285
Tom Kite	73	67	72	73	285
Billy Casper	71	76	71	69	287
Roger Maltbie	72	75	70	71	288
Graham Marsh	73	68	75	72	288
Tom Weiskopf	73	71	70	74	288
Jim Colbert	71	72	74	72	289
Lou Graham	68	73	72	76	289
Gene Littler	71	72	74	72	289
Al Geiberger	75	70	73	73	291
Dave Hill	69	73	76	73	291
Jerry McGee	71	73	72	75	291
Curtis Strange	71	76	73	71	291
Bud Allin	69	76	72	75	292
Bruce Devlin	77	69	72	74	292
Hubert Green	71	66	78	77	292
Dale Hayes	75	74	73	70	292
Gay Brewer	75	74	71	73	293
Rik Massengale	70	72	78	73	293
Johnny Miller	71	73	74	75	293
Peter Oosterhuis	76	74	75	68	293

Index

184

CHAMPIONSHIP CARD

HOLE	YARDS	PAR
1	400	4
2	555	5
3	360	4
4	220	3
5	450	4
6	190	3
7	365	4
8	530	5
9	440	4
OUT	3510	36
10	485	4
11	445	4
12	155	3
13	485	5
14	420	4
15	520	5
16	190	3
17	400	4
18	420	4
IN	3520	36
TOTAL	7030	72